3 Colour in the picture you have drawn.

4 Write your name underneath.

Fill in everything about yourself!

Question time!
Do you look like your Mum or Dad?

5 I am a [blank] *girl / boy*

6 I am [blank] years old

7 My birthday is the [blank]

8 My hair is [blank] *brown / blonde / red / black*

9 My hair is [blank] *short / straight / curly / long*

10 My eyes are [blank] *grey / green / brown / blue*

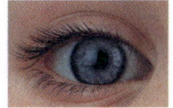 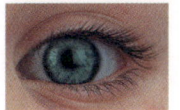 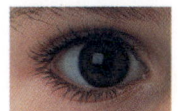 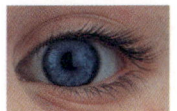

My family

11 How many people are there in your family?

12 Circle the people that are in your family.

mother

grandfather

stepmother

uncle

stepfather

sister

brother

aunt

cousin

grandmother

father

13 Draw a picture of the oldest person in your family.

14 Draw a picture of the youngest person in your family.

My friends

15 Write the name of your best friend, or your best friends if you have lots!

16 Tick the boxes of the activities that you like to do with your friends.

☐ Eat lunch together ☐ Dance at a party ☐ Play football in a team

☐ Tell jokes to each other ☐ Paint fun pictures ☐ Swim in the pool

My secret club

17 Invite some friends to join your secret club, and write their names here.

18 Look at this secret code. Can you use it to help you decode the message below?

A ● B ♥ C ⬠ D ■ E ⚡ F ◗ G ■

H ★ I ◗ J ◖ K ▲ L ◖ M ♥ N ★

O ■ P ▲ Q ● R ◗ S ★ T ■ U ▲

V ⚡ W ● X ◖ Y ♥ Z ⚡

♥ ⚡ ★ ■   ◗ ◗ ◗ ⚡ ★ ■ ★

— — — —   — — — — — — —

19 Use the code to write a message for the members of your secret club.

20 Make up your own special code by drawing a symbol, number or letter next to each letter of the alphabet.

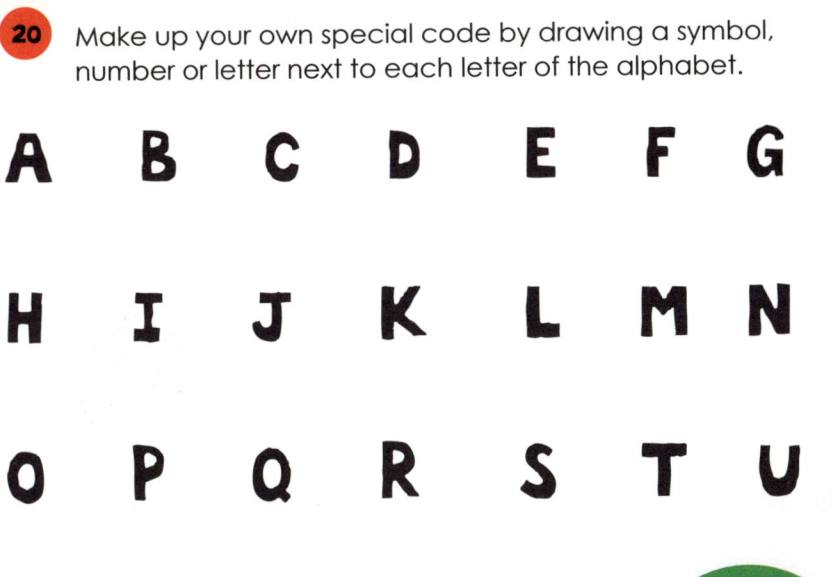

A   B   C   D   E   F   G

H   I   J   K   L   M   N

O   P   Q   R   S   T   U

V   W   X   Y   Z

Question time!
How many of your friends are members of your secret club?

21 Write your name in your special code.

22 Think of a password for your secret club members, and write it in your special code.

My pets

23 Do you have a pet? What is it called?

Trace over the names of the pets, then draw lines to match the names to the pictures.

24 cat

25 rabbit

26 mouse

27 horse

28 dog

29 fish

30 Draw a picture of your favourite animal.

31 Colour in the picture.

32 Write the animal's name underneath.

Question time!
Which pet makes a "meow" sound?

At school

33 There are people in my class at school.

Draw lines to match the pictures to the sentences about travelling to school.

34

I travel to school in a bus.

35

I ride to school on my bike.

36

I go to school in a car.

37

I walk to school.

Trace over the words to write the subjects.

38 reading

39 art

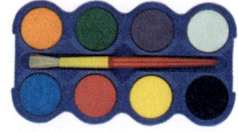

40 geography

41 maths

Question time!
Which subject do you find easy? Which do you find hard?

42 Which subject do you enjoy the most?

43 Who is your favourite teacher?

Musical instruments

44 Do you play a musical instrument? Which one?

45 Which is your favourite musical instrument?

Use the pictures and descriptions to help you work out the instrument names from the mixed-up letters.

46 This is a silver instrument which you blow into.

elfut

47 This instrument has black and white keys.

panio

48 You hit this instrument with sticks to make a sound.

rdum

49 You use a bow to make a sound with this instrument.

vonili

Can you find the musical instruments in the word search?

i	f	o	e	n	a	f	m	a	y	t	a	t
v	i	o	l	i	n	o	l	c	e	l	l	o
x	a	o	p	x	d	f	a	o	i	f	p	n
h	e	x	y	l	o	p	h	o	n	e	a	g
t	t	a	i	g	u	i	a	t	l	e	n	h
d	r	u	m	a	r	a	g	c	e	l	a	o
d	u	a	t	h	g	n	a	y	a	d	y	x
u	m	i	s	e	d	o	f	m	i	f	a	p
m	p	f	p	o	a	l	l	p	x	l	l	s
a	e	e	n	d	u	d	t	a	o	u	a	p
g	t	i	a	g	g	t	g	u	i	t	a	r
r	w	p	u	x	f	a	n	h	x	e	o	d

50 xylophone

51 violin

52 guitar

53 flute

54 piano

55 trumpet

56 drum

57 cello

Sports I play

58 What is your favourite sport?

Trace over the names of the sports, then tick the boxes of the sports you enjoy.

59 ice hockey ☐

60 tennis ☐

61 football ☐

62 gymnastics ☐

63 basketball ☐

64 golf ☐

Can you find the football words in the word search?

a	s	o	t	r	w	h	f	t	a	p	b	a
w	l	r	y	g	a	o	l	a	y	g	b	w
h	t	p	b	f	w	s	l	b	t	a	o	f
i	f	o	a	l	a	h	a	p	r	a	o	h
s	s	h	t	a	r	g	w	b	o	f	t	a
t	a	a	g	g	s	a	s	a	p	h	s	p
l	a	w	a	a	p	i	t	c	h	l	w	o
e	b	h	t	y	o	a	l	b	y	r	a	o
h	f	b	p	o	t	g	w	s	y	h	t	l
a	s	a	l	l	f	b	g	l	o	v	e	s
p	o	l	h	s	h	o	r	t	s	t	a	f
t	o	l	t	r	p	a	o	s	b	a	o	h

65 pitch **66** whistle  **67** boots **68** flag

69 trophy  **70** ball **71** shorts  **72** gloves

When I grow up...

73 What job, or jobs, do you think you might like to do when you grow up?

74 What job does your Mum or Dad do?

Read the job descriptions, then circle the words that finish the sentences.

75

Firefighters save lives by rescuing people and putting out...

candles

fires

76

People who work for the police make sure the streets are...

safe

clean

77

Dentists look after people's teeth and...

hair

gums

78

Teachers teach subjects to children who are called their...

students

babies

79

Zookeepers look after many different types of animals in the...

sea

zoo

80

Mechanics fix all kinds of vehicles with their...

tools

friends

81

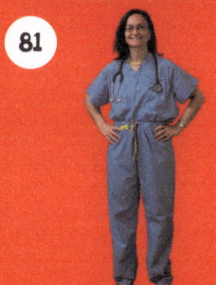

Midwives look after pregnant ladies, and help them....

give birth

bake

82

Gardeners look after gardens. They like to plant...

flowers

cars

83

Vets take care of animals when they are...

hungry

sick

Can you find the names of the jobs in the word search? Tick the boxes when you find them.

z	a	f	i	r	e	f	i	g	h	t	e	r
o	i	p	c	t	a	n	g	z	g	f	a	k
o	k	e	g	f	i	k	a	r	v	e	t	e
k	f	c	t	a	k	a	r	d	n	p	i	t
e	g	a	m	p	m	i	d	w	i	f	e	a
e	n	p	t	e	e	i	e	f	m	a	g	f
p	i	a	e	k	m	a	n	a	t	n	z	k
e	g	t	a	c	p	d	e	n	t	i	s	t
r	e	p	c	e	n	a	r	t	a	m	e	i
n	f	a	h	c	g	f	i	a	p	g	n	v
a	g	m	e	c	h	a	n	i	c	a	z	e
f	e	a	r	p	i	t	f	i	c	k	f	a

84 firefighter **85** teacher **86** mechanic **87** dentist

88 zookeeper **89** gardener **90** midwife **91** vet

Learn about the world

Discover all about different countries,
planet Earth, space and more.

92 Colour in the Earth when you are ready to start this section.

North America

93 Look at the map, then trace over the name of the continent.

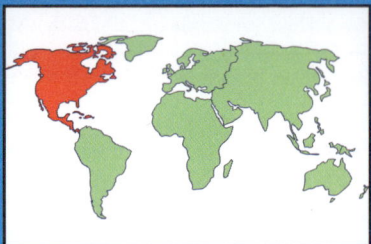

North
America

94 Look at the flag of the United States, then count the stripes and write the numbers in the boxes.

white stripes [ ] red stripes [ ]

95 Mexican food often contains chillies. Circle the word that describes how chillies make food taste.

spicy   salty   sweet

96 Grizzly bears live in North America. Can you fill in the missing letters?

g _ i z _ l y
_ _ a r

Can you find the countries in the word search? Tick the boxes when you find them.

h	o	n	d	u	r	a	s	a	g	p	j	g
l	y	e	d	h	v	r	f	x	t	c	n	u
q	b	w	a	j	a	m	a	i	c	a	r	a
y	a	p	m	e	s	j	v	c	d	n	z	t
c	h	s	n	c	u	b	a	i	z	a	c	e
q	a	k	f	b	t	r	l	w	t	d	i	m
u	m	d	m	e	x	i	c	o	n	a	w	a
o	a	u	a	k	g	m	s	p	b	o	k	l
h	s	x	b	c	o	s	t	a	r	i	c	a

97 Bahamas **98** Honduras **99** Jamaica **100** Cuba

101 Guatemala **102** Canada **103** Costa Rica **104** Mexico

105 The city of New Orleans in the United States is famous for jazz music. What is this instrument called?

t _ _ m _ _ _

Africa

106 Look at the continent of Africa, then trace over its name.

Africa

Can you find the animals in the word search?

r	h	i	n	o	c	e	r	o	s	b	f	l
d	u	q	w	c	i	p	f	u	r	z	g	m
l	t	k	i	e	t	y	c	n	l	o	i	v
e	l	e	p	h	a	n	t	e	i	d	r	e
o	y	l	g	r	x	h	j	s	o	h	a	j
p	o	z	e	b	r	a	l	p	n	z	f	a
a	n	s	a	m	g	i	s	a	t	v	f	h
r	g	b	r	x	b	p	m	o	n	k	e	y
d	c	t	i	g	e	r	f	k	q	d	w	a

107  rhinoceros **108** monkey **109** lion **110**  zebra

111 elephant **112** leopard **113** giraffe **114** tiger

115 Trace over the name of the highest mountain in Africa.

Mount Kilimanjaro

116 Camels can survive for up to two weeks without drinking any water. Where do camels live?

In the jungle   In the desert   In the sea

117 Join the dots to draw the rhinoceros.

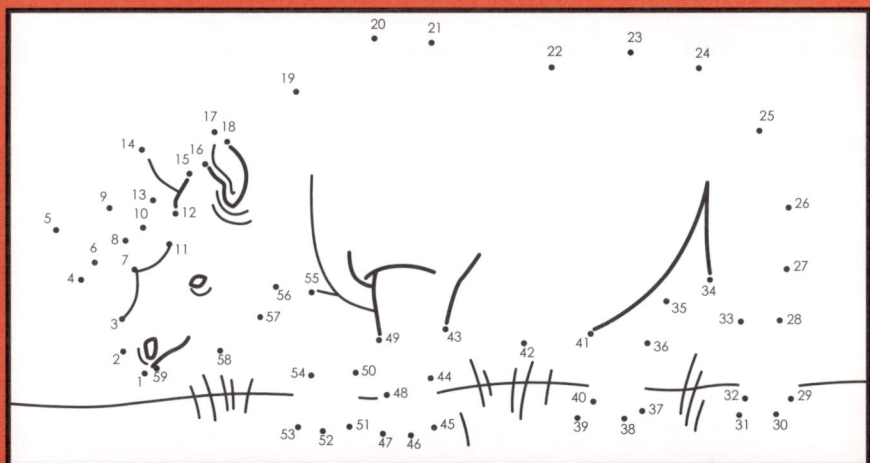

118 Fill in the missing letters to spell the name of these ancient monuments in Egypt.

P _ r _ m _ d s

South America

119 Look at the map, then trace over the name of the continent.

South
America

120 These statues were found on an island near Chile called Easter Island. How many statues can you count in the picture?

7   9

12   5

121 Can you circle the name of the islands where the giant Galapagos tortoises live?

The Galapagos Islands   The Shetland Islands

122 This is an ancient city in Peru that was built by people called the Incas. Can you trace over the name?

Machu Picchu

123 Colour in the flag of Chile.

124 Trace over the name of this South American animal.

llama

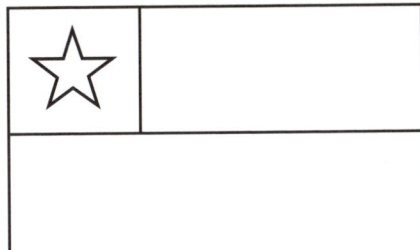

125 Can you find a way to lead the ball to the Brazilian football shirt?

Draw lines to match the sentences to the places.

126 The largest mountain range in the world is called the...

Amazon

127 The largest rainforest in South America is called the...

Andes

Europe

128 Look at the continent of Europe, then trace over its name.

Europe

Learn your capital cities! Then trace over the country names.

129 Rome is the capital city of

Italy

130 London is the capital city of

England

131 Athens is the capital city of

Greece

132 Colour in the flag of Germany.

133 The Eiffel Tower is a very famous landmark in Paris, France. Circle the word that describes it.

| tall | short | colourful |

Question time! Can you think of the names of any other countries in Europe?

Fill in the missing letters of the foods that are made in Italy.

134

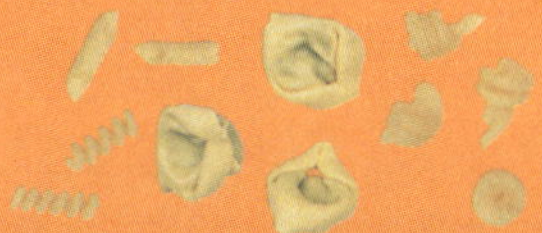

_ _ s t _

135

p _ _ _ a

136 Stonehenge is a monument in England that dates back to around 3,000 BC. It is very...

| old | new |

137 Look at the Spanish flag, then write the colours that are in it.

_ _ _   _ _ _ _ _ _

138 Fill in the missing word in this sentence.

Fish and _____ is a popular dish in the United Kingdom.

Asia

139 Look at the map, then trace over the name of the continent.

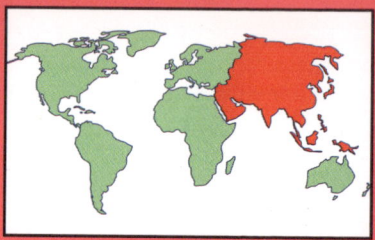

Asia

Draw lines to match the facts to the pictures.

140 The Great Wall of China is the longest wall in the world.

141 The Taj Mahal is a very famous and beautiful building in India.

142 Mount Everest is the tallest mountain in the world.

143 Can you trace over the letters to write the name of the Japanese dish?

sushi

144 Can you circle the name of this fruit that grows in Thailand?

pineapple   pear

145 Circle the trail that leads the chopsticks to the bowl of rice.

146 Can you circle the food that pandas love to eat?

soup   bamboo

147 Trace over the name of the highest mountain in the world.

Mount Everest

148 Colour in the picture of Mount Everest.

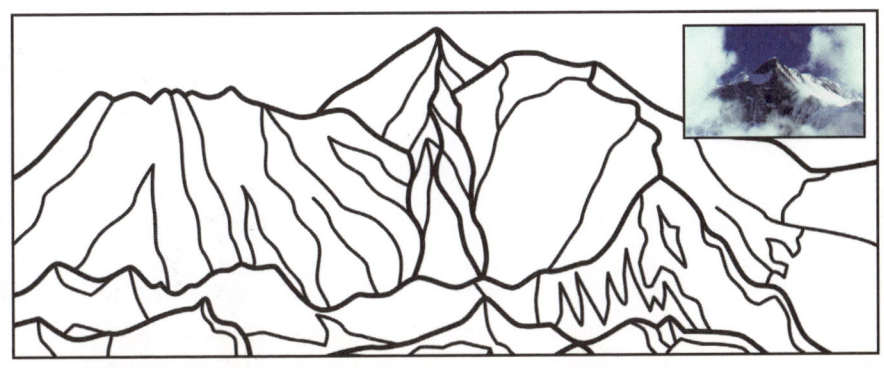

Australia and New Zealand

149 Look at the map of Australia and New Zealand, then trace over the name.

Australia

150 This Australian building is called the Sydney Opera House. Can you join the dots to draw it?

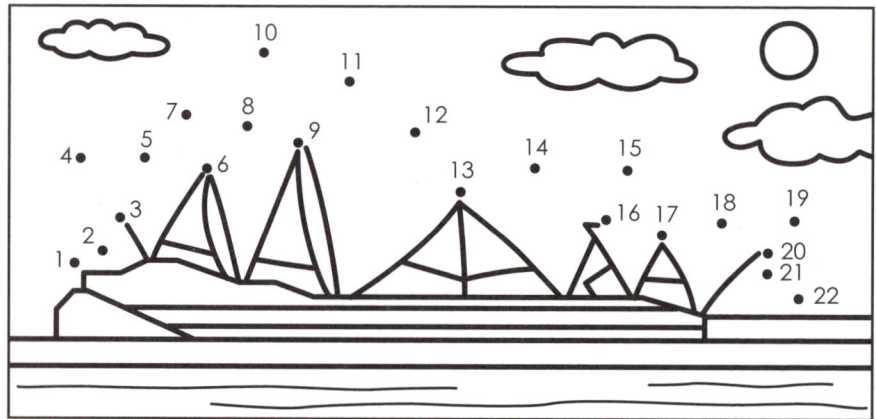

151 Circle the country that kiwi fruits come from.

New Zealand   Australia

152 What is the name of the animal that carries her baby in her pouch?

k _ n _ _ _ o o

153 Colour in the flag of New Zealand.

Count the sheep, rugby balls, boomerangs and kiwi fruits and write the totals in the boxes.

154 sheep   **155** rugby balls   **156** boomerangs   **157** kiwi fruits

The Earth

Draw lines to match the pictures to the descriptions of the things we get from Earth.

158 These precious stones are dug out of the ground.

159 This material is mined from rocks and made into things such as keys.

160 These grow on the ground and are made into food.

161 Circle the trail that leads the orange to the orange juice.

a

b

c

162 Trace over the name of this red fruit.

strawberry

Use the pictures to help you write the names using the mixed-up letters. Then colour in the pictures.

Did you know? All our tasty fruits and vegetables grow on or in the ground.

163 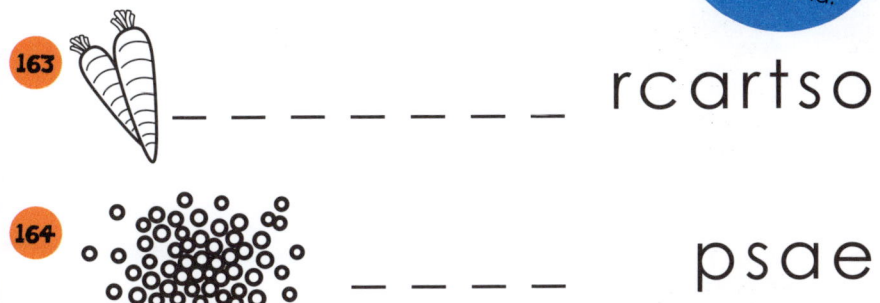 _ _ _ _ _ _ _   rcartso

164 _ _ _ _   psae

165 _ _ _ _ _   lppae

166 _ _ _ _ _ _   gprsae

167 _ _ _ _ _ _   geoarn

168 _ _ _ _ _ _ _   anbanas

The Earth

Can you trace over the words to complete the sentences below?

169
Bees collect nectar from flowers and make it into

honey

170
Cows eat grass to help them make

milk

171
Trees are turned into

paper

Question time!
What do hens lay that we eat in lots of different ways?

172
Rainforest plants are made into

medicines

173
Crops, such as wheat, are made into bread and

cereals

Look at the pictures of some of the things that we get from the Earth. Can you find their names in the word search?

b	k	i	v	e	g	e	t	a	b	l	e	s
g	o	u	p	s	d	t	m	z	j	w	l	p
m	d	o	s	f	l	o	w	e	r	s	r	c
y	i	h	z	k	c	b	g	q	n	x	f	u
p	a	l	f	r	u	i	t	s	x	r	u	m
f	m	x	c	a	q	v	j	d	a	o	d	e
w	o	o	d	o	y	e	t	z	t	c	h	t
v	n	y	i	k	l	r	j	w	r	k	n	a
r	d	v	f	w	a	t	e	r	a	s	g	l
a	s	h	s	b	m	i	e	q	w	n	t	s

 **174** vegetables

 **175** water

 **176** flowers

 **177** metals

 **178** diamonds

 **179** fruits

 **180** wood

 **181** rocks

Space

Trace over the names of the planets in our Solar System.

182  Mercury

183 Venus

184 Earth

185 Mars

186 Jupiter

187 Saturn

188 Uranus

189 Neptune

Earth is the only planet with life. This is because we have air and water on Earth, and heat and light from the Sun. Can you unscramble the letters to spell the four things that make life possible on Earth?

190 ria

_ _ _

191 ghlit

_ _ _ _ _

192 htae

_ _ _ _

193 twaer

_ _ _ _ _

194 Can you spot five differences between the two astronauts? Circle these on picture B.

A

B

Space

Can you find the space words in the word search? Tick the boxes when you find them.

d	x	m	o	o	n	c	w	b	t	u	o	i
a	q	h	l	n	z	g	q	e	h	z	k	n
s	k	w	y	g	u	n	i	v	e	r	s	e
t	s	a	t	n	r	d	x	q	a	s	g	c
r	j	v	s	u	n	l	j	x	r	l	u	e
o	p	f	p	h	t	m	r	d	t	b	p	v
n	b	y	c	s	q	v	a	o	h	k	l	i
a	s	r	j	t	e	j	s	p	m	e	a	q
u	o	i	g	a	l	a	x	y	i	g	n	a
t	f	m	p	r	d	f	r	v	b	o	e	w
j	a	u	t	z	m	h	n	k	c	y	t	l

195 astronaut **196** star **197** galaxy **198** Moon

199 universe **200** Earth **201** planet **202** Sun

203 A constellation is the name given to a pattern of stars. Can you join the stars to draw the constellation of The Great Bear?

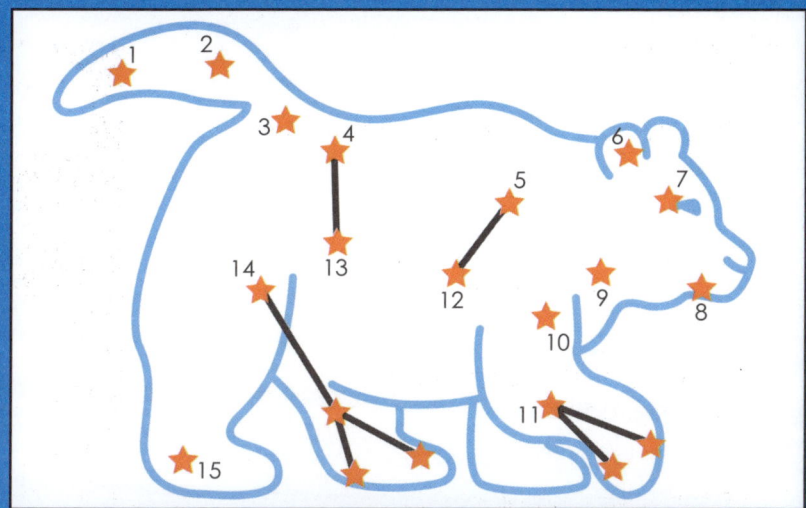

There are about one billion planets in our galaxy. Trace over the numbers to get an idea of how many a billion is!

204 1 0 0   one hundred

205 1,000   one thousand

206 1,000,000,000   one billion

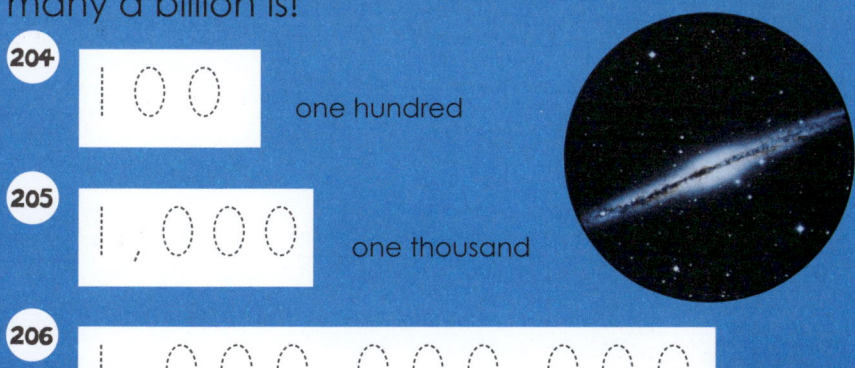

Space

Draw lines to match the pictures to the descriptions.

207 People who are trained to travel into space are called astronauts.

208 Satellites are sent into space to carry out research.

209 Shooting stars are small bits of burning rock.

210 Earth is the only planet that can support life.

211 Neptune is a very stormy planet, with winds that blow really fast.

Unscramble the letters to write the names of two of the planets in our Solar System.

212 _ _ _ _ _ _ _ pjuiter

213 _ _ _ _ _ _ tunsar

214 Can you colour the planets in our Solar System, and the Sun too?

215 Can you join the dots to draw the space shuttle?

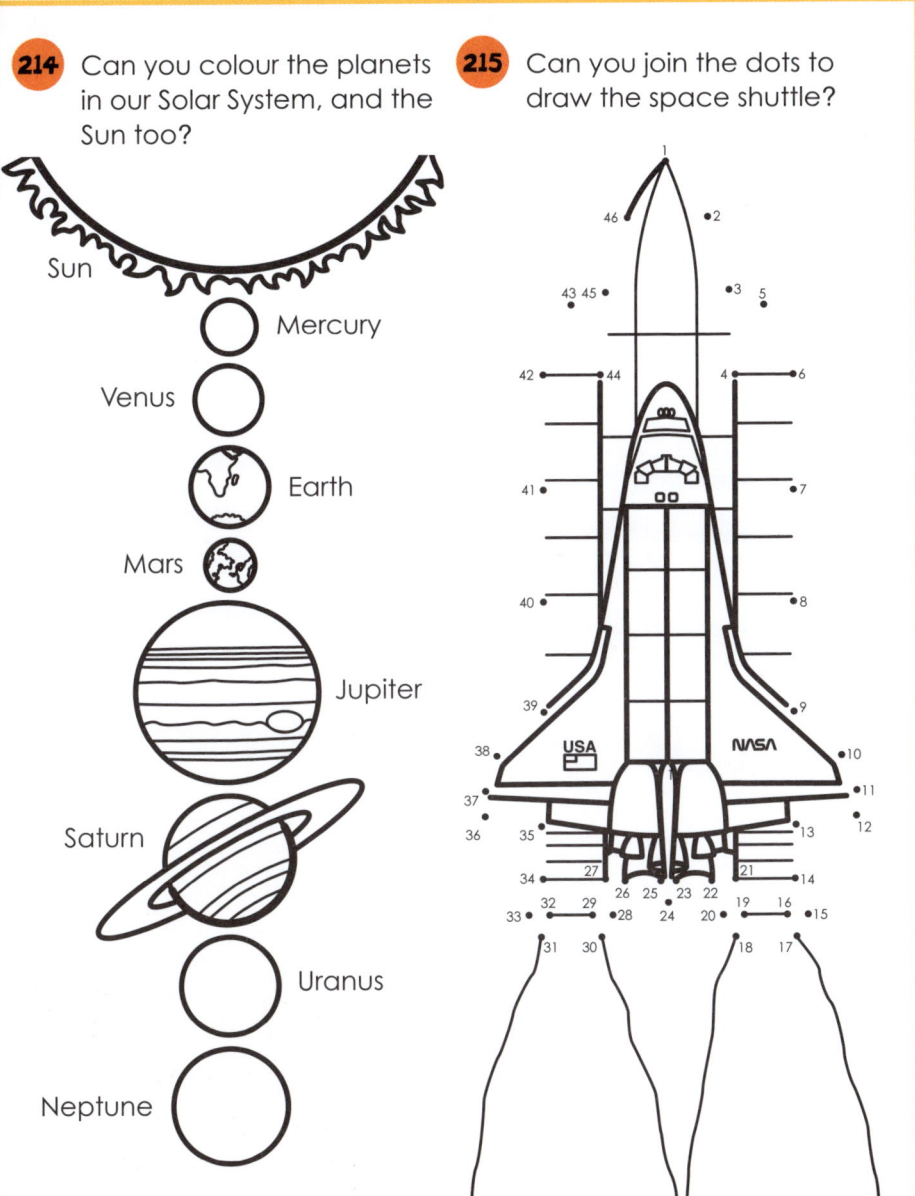

Sun

Mercury

Venus

Earth

Mars

Jupiter

Saturn

Uranus

Neptune

USA

NASA

Rainforests

216 Can you trace over the name of the huge rainforest which is in South America?

Amazon rainforest

217 Join the dots to draw this animal that lives in the rainforest.

Did you know?
Monkeys screech loudly as they swing through the trees.

218 Colour in the scene.

219 Fill in the missing letters to write the animal's name.

m _ _ k _ _

220 Huge spiders such as the Goliath tarantula live in rainforests. How many legs does this spider have?

2   4   6   8

221 Can you colour this poison arrow frog blue?

Draw lines to match the pictures to the descriptions.

222

Many rainforest plants are made into medicines which help people feel better when they are ill.

223

My strong, hooked bill helps me to open tough nuts.

Deserts

Can you find the desert words in the word search?

a	m	q	e	t	d	e	s	e	r	t	w	n
h	x	c	j	b	y	e	d	n	c	d	p	e
w	c	l	a	o	a	s	i	s	j	o	l	h
i	a	g	v	b	c	n	g	q	m	y	i	a
z	c	i	e	s	z	a	o	r	d	f	z	u
p	t	d	s	m	u	k	j	h	r	t	a	f
z	u	o	w	l	d	e	b	f	y	n	r	k
g	s	a	n	d	f	l	n	s	g	k	d	x
k	e	c	r	i	y	h	o	t	p	v	a	b

224 desert   **225** dry   **226** hot   **227** lizard

228 cactus   **229** sand   **230** snake   **231** oasis

232  Camels from Africa have one hump, and camels from Asia have two. Can you write where this camel is from?

_ _ _ _ _ _

233 Can you unscramble these letters to write the name of the world's largest desert?

a s r h a a   d e e r s t

s _ h _ _ a   d _ s _ _ t

234 Circle the word that describes what a cactus feels like.

spiky   smooth

Can you fill in the missing letters to spell the names of these desert animals?

235 a n _ _ l _ _ e

236 c _ m _ l

237 l _ z _ r d

238 s _ _ k e

Coral reefs

 239 Trace over the name of the largest coral reef in the world. It stretches for about 2,000 km off the coast of Australia.

Great Barrier Reef

240 Can you spot five differences between these coral reef scenes? Circle these on picture B.

A

B

 241 Octopuses use their arms for swimming, gripping prey and fighting. How many arms does an octopus have?

2   4   6   8

Draw lines to match the pictures to the descriptions.

242

This fish is covered in slime so it is not stung when it hides in sea anemones' tentacles.

243

This shark hunts on the coral reef for small fish to eat.

244

Most starfish have five arms, but some can have as many as 50 arms!

245 Can you join the dots to draw the starfish?

The Arctic

The Arctic is a huge area of frozen ice that surrounds the North Pole. Can you find the eight Arctic words in the word search?

d	x	p	o	l	a	r	b	e	a	r	o	i
f	q	h	l	s	e	a	q	e	r	z	k	n
r	k	i	y	g	u	n	i	v	c	r	s	e
o	s	c	t	n	r	d	x	q	t	s	w	c
z	j	e	s	u	n	l	j	x	i	l	a	e
e	p	f	p	h	t	m	r	d	c	b	l	i
n	b	y	c	s	q	v	a	o	f	k	r	n
a	s	r	j	t	e	j	s	p	o	e	u	u
w	o	l	v	e	r	i	n	e	x	g	s	i
t	f	m	p	r	d	f	r	v	b	o	e	t

246 frozen

247 Arctic fox

248 sea

249 ice

250 polar bear

251 Inuit

252 wolverine

253 walrus

254 Can you join the dots to draw the polar bear?

255 Now write the animal's name.

polar bear

256 How many tusks does a walrus have?

3   1   2   4

257 Can you unscramble these letters to write the name of the pole that is in the Arctic?

orhtn lope

n _ r _ h   _ o _ e

Did you know?
People who live in the Arctic are called by two names – Inuit or Eskimo.

Antarctica

Antarctica is a large continent at the most southern point of the world.

258 Can you unscramble these letters to write the name of the pole that is in Antarctica?

t u o s h   p l e o

s _ _ t _   p _ l _

259 Penguins huddle together in groups to keep warm. How many penguins can you count in this scene?

260 Can you trace over the name of this type of whale that lives in Antarctica?

killer whale

Circle the words that complete these sentences.

261 Temperatures in Antarctica reach as low as -80° Celcius. That is very...

cold   hot

262 During the summer in Antarctica the sun does not set, so it never gets...

light   dark

263 Most of Antarctica is covered by a sheet of ice, which in some places is up to 4 kilometres thick. That is very...

deep   thin

264 Can you circle the penguin that is different from all the others?

 a
 b
 c
 d

world map

Draw lines from the names of the continents to where they appear on the map.

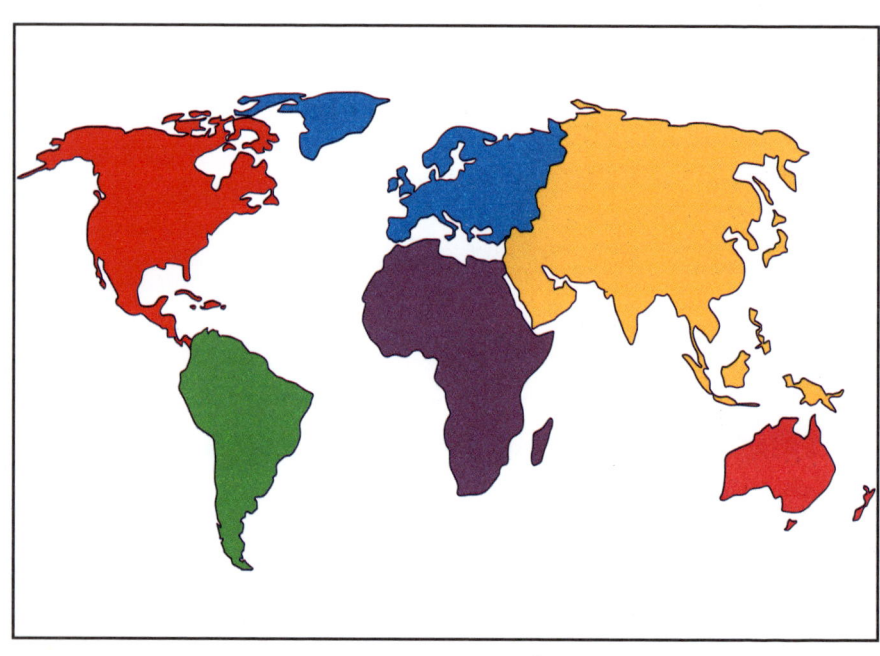

265 Africa

266 Europe

267 North America

268 Asia

269 South America

270 Australia and New Zealand

The human body

Learn all about your amazing body!

Colour in the picture when you are ready to start this section.

My body

Fill in the missing letters to label the parts of the body.

272 h _ _ d

273 _ e _ k

274 _ r _

275 h _ p

276 h _ _ d

277 k n _ _

278 l _ _

279 a _ k _ _

280 t _ _ s

281 _ o _ t

Question time!
Have you ever broken a bone in your body?

Fill in the missing words to complete the sentences about what our bodies can do!

stretch	jump	kick	bend	bounce	splits

282 Our bodies can _____ into a crab.

283 We can _____ really high!

284 Some people can do the _____ .

285 We can _____ around.

286 We can _____ a ball.

287 We can _____ .

Question time!
What do you do on a trampoline?

Super senses

Our bodies have five senses. Fill in the missing letters to write the names of these.

288 T _ u _ h

290

289 S _ _ ll

291

H _ _ r _ n g

292

T _ s _ e

Si _ _ t

293 Which of your five senses do you use when you read a book?

294 Which of your five senses do you use when you listen to music?

Draw lines to match the pictures to the descriptions.

295 The tongue is made up of taste buds. Different parts of the tongue taste different things.

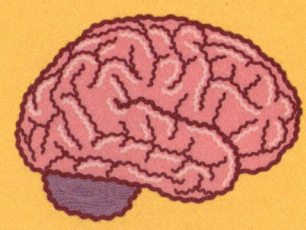

296 The brain is the body's computer. It controls everything that your body does, from moving and talking to thinking and remembering.

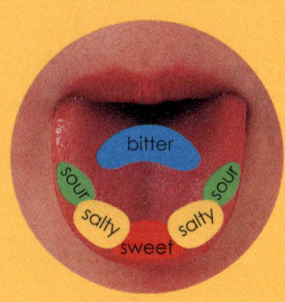

Circle the words that describe how these children are feeling.

297
scared
silly

298
angry
surprised

299
upset
happy

300
shy
excited

Body fuel

Draw lines to match the pictures to the types of foods that they are.

301

302

303

304

305

meat

vegetables

fruit

grains

dairy foods

Can you find the body words in the word search?
Tick the boxes when you find them.

s	b	l	o	o	d	o	t	r	h	g	w	s
f	m	w	k	y	u	l	z	k	u	f	d	t
u	u	s	l	i	v	e	r	j	x	c	r	o
i	s	e	r	h	u	i	t	t	h	n	j	m
b	c	a	d	l	b	n	u	p	l	o	i	a
r	l	u	i	u	d	v	e	h	m	f	g	c
a	e	w	p	n	x	c	m	e	c	h	q	h
i	s	w	s	g	d	e	w	a	u	o	p	p
n	m	w	l	s	h	t	s	r	e	r	l	k
k	p	g	d	d	y	i	j	t	l	b	r	k
i	o	q	e	w	l	k	b	o	n	e	s	d
y	o	e	r	u	w	f	v	c	x	z	s	a

 **306** muscles

 **307** heart

 308 blood

 309 lungs

310 stomach

 **311** liver

312 bones

313 brain

Parts of your body

314 Draw a picture of yourself in the frame.

315 Label as many parts of your body as you can.

316 Colour in the picture.

Things that go

Learn about giant machines, speedy trains and lots more.

 317 Colour in the aeroplanes when you are ready to start this section.

Giant machines

Draw lines to match the pictures to the descriptions.

318 Giant excavators have huge caterpillar tracks, which are as tall as a man.

319 Backhoe loaders dig with their backhoe and scoop up earth with their bucket.

320 Concrete trucks mix concrete in their turning drum, and then pour this to make roads and more.

321 Dump trucks can carry huge amounts of earth and rock.

322 Join the dots to draw the giant excavator.

323 Colour in the picture.

Speedy machines

Draw lines to match the pictures to the descriptions.

324 Racing cars are very light, and reach super speeds of up to 370 km/hour.

325 4x4 trucks have large wheels. They are very powerful.

326 Quad bikes have strong suspensions, and can travel over all terrains.

327 Superbikes can reach amazing speeds of over 300 km/hour.

Can you find the machine words in the word search? Tick the boxes when you find them.

i	f	o	e	n	g	i	n	e	y	t	a	s
v	e	p	o	w	n	o	i	e	g	p	i	t
w	a	g	p	s	d	f	a	o	i	s	a	e
h	h	x	o	p	o	w	e	r	t	u	g	e
e	t	a	i	o	u	i	n	t	l	s	n	r
e	r	r	m	w	r	a	g	c	e	p	i	s
l	u	a	t	m	a	c	h	i	n	e	y	h
s	m	b	s	e	d	o	a	m	i	n	a	p
m	p	r	m	o	a	e	e	p	a	s	l	i
n	g	a	n	d	u	r	d	a	o	i	s	u
g	t	k	a	s	p	e	e	d	i	o	a	w
r	w	e	u	s	f	a	w	h	i	n	o	d

328 speed   **329** machine   **330** engine   **331** power

332 suspension   **333** wheels   **334** steer   **335** brake

On the water

Draw lines to match the pictures to the descriptions.

336 In canoes, people use a paddle to steer and move through the water.

337 Powerboats reach speeds of 130 km/hour, and when they travel fast the front of the boat lifts up.

338 Police boats are used by the police for patrolling coastlines and other areas.

339 Cruise ships take people around the world. Some are so big that they have swimming pools on board!

Count how many police boats, cruise ships, ferries and sailing boats there are, then write the totals in the boxes.

340 Police boats ▢

341 Ferries ▢

342 Cruise ships ▢

343 Sailing boats ▢

Amazing machines

Draw lines to match the pictures to the descriptions.

344 Huge container ships transport many different types of goods all around the world.

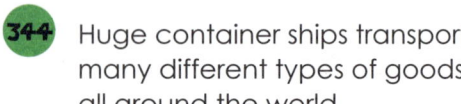

345 Bullet trains can carry more than 1,300 passengers, and travel at up to 300 km/hour.

346 Space shuttles are huge machines that travel into space at super speeds.

347 Jumbo jets are so big, they can carry up to 600 passengers.

348 Colour in the airport scene.

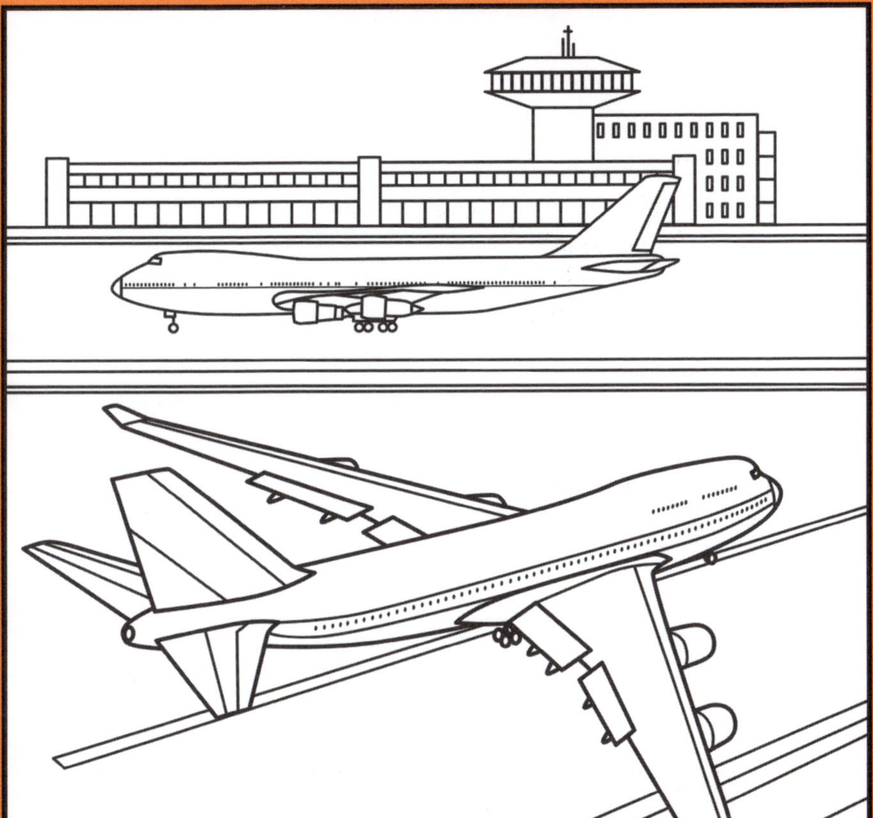

349 Have you ever travelled in an aeroplane? Where did you fly to?

Missing letters

Fill in the missing letters to write the names of the things that go.

350

d _ _ _
_ r _ c _

351

_ a _ _ e

352

_ _ n _ r _ t _
t _ u _ _

353

r _ _ i _ _
c _ r

354

_ p _ _ e

s _ u _ _ l _

Question time!
Which machine do you travel in to fly into space?

355

q u _ _

_ _ k _

356

c r _ _ _ _

_ _ i _

357

s _ p _ r _ i _ e

Counting things that go

Count the concrete trucks, racing cars, canoes and jumbo jets and write the totals in the boxes.

358	Concrete trucks	
359	Racing cars	
360	Canoes	
361	Jumbo jets	

Discovering dinosaurs

Learn all about the different types of dinosaurs.

 362 Colour in the picture of Triceratops when you are ready to start this section.

Meat-eating dinosaurs

Trace over the names of the meat-eating dinos.

363 Tyrannosaurus rex

364 Velociraptor

365 Allosaurus

366 Troodon

Carnotauru

Did you know? We find out about dinosaurs by studying their fossils.

367 Baryonyx liked to eat fish. Can you circle the trail that leads to the fish?

A B C

Can you find the dino words in the word search?
Tick the boxes when you find them.

h	u	i	b	x	w	q	w	j	p	u	w	t
o	q	w	e	w	v	t	a	i	l	w	f	i
r	w	p	a	i	p	u	k	h	f	s	s	h
n	z	l	k	h	k	i	f	l	a	p	w	j
s	h	k	w	f	g	p	k	w	s	i	h	l
j	j	c	c	l	a	w	s	g	a	k	m	j
g	y	b	w	l	m	g	h	v	g	e	g	c
s	e	a	q	r	k	j	a	w	o	s	k	h
m	d	i	n	o	s	a	u	r	t	e	r	a
w	r	a	u	y	w	t	e	t	d	d	s	r
o	f	r	h	d	w	j	d	t	m	k	l	g
i	l	t	e	e	t	h	k	q	a	e	i	e

368 teeth
369 horns
370 tail
371 charge
372 spikes
373 claws
374 dinosaur
375 beak

Plant-eating dinosaurs

Read the dinosaur names, then practise saying them!

376 **Diplodocus**
Di-PLOD-uh-kus

377 **Ultrasaurus**
UL-trah-SAWR-us

378 **Iguanodon**
Ig-WAN-oh-DON

379 **Hadrosaurus**
HAD-roh-SAWR-us

380 **Chasmosaurus**
CHAS-mo-SAWR-us

381 **Triceratops**
TRI-seh-ruh-TOPS

Did you know?
In 1858 Hadrosaurus was the first dinosaur to be discovered in North America.

Iguanodon

382 Chasmosaurus had a large frill on its neck. How many horns did it have?

| 2 | 5 | 3 |

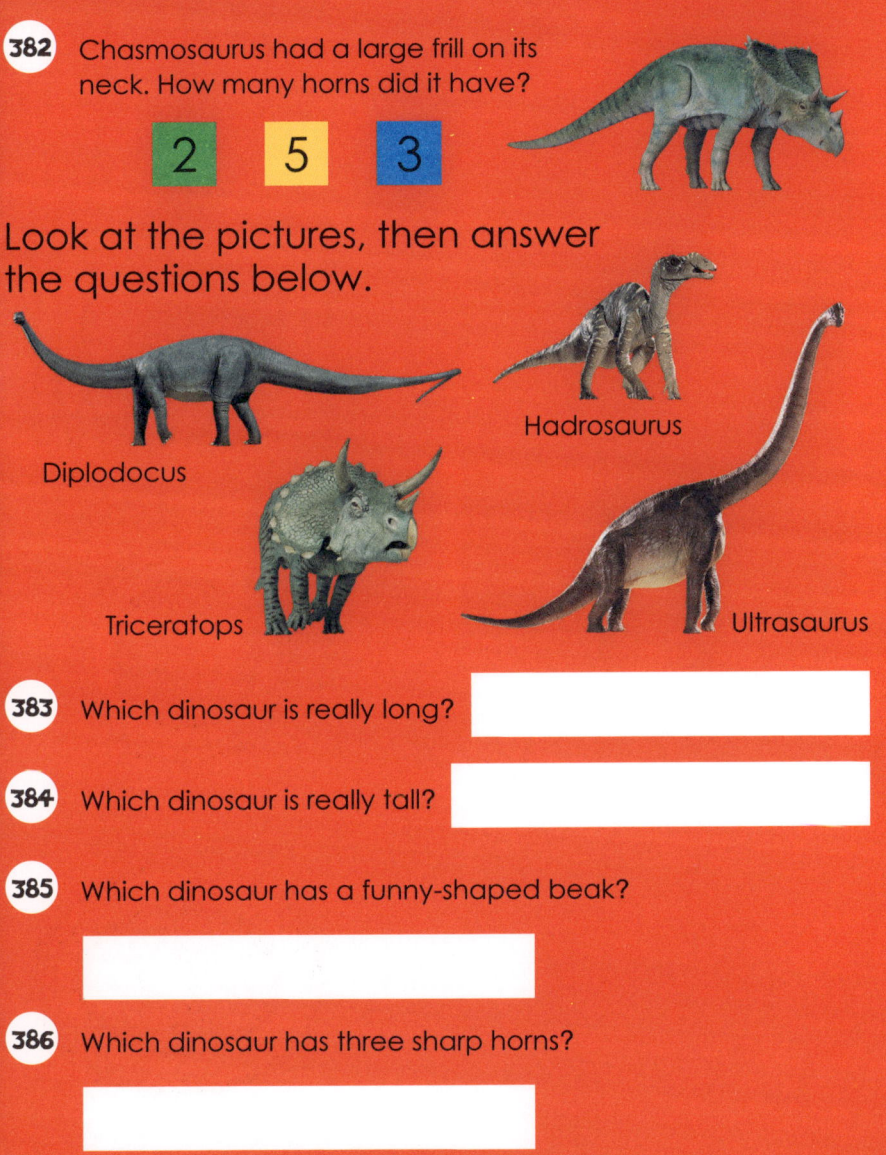

Look at the pictures, then answer the questions below.

Diplodocus

Hadrosaurus

Triceratops

Ultrasaurus

383 Which dinosaur is really long?

384 Which dinosaur is really tall?

385 Which dinosaur has a funny-shaped beak?

386 Which dinosaur has three sharp horns?

Dinosaur gallery

Read about these dinosaurs, colour in the picture frames and fill in the missing letters to write their names.

387 Euoplocephalus was covered in bony plates and had a club at the end of its tail.

388 E _ o p _ _ c e _ h _ l u s

389 Gravitholus had a thick, heavy skull. These dinosaurs may have charged head first in fights.

390 G r _ v _ t _ _ l u _

391 Triceratops had three sharp horns and a large, bony frill behind its neck.

392 T _ i c e _ _ t _ p s

393 Kentrosaurus had spikes along its back and tail. It had a very small brain, so wasn't a clever dinosaur!

394 K _ n t _ o _ a _ r u s

395 Nodosaurus had lots of tough, knobbly plates along its back. Its name means 'lumpy reptile'.

396 N o _ _ s a _ r _ s

397 Parasaurolophus had a crazy, hollow crest on its head which it probably used to make sounds.

398 P a _ a _ a _ r o l _ p h _ s

Dinosaur gallery

399 Tyrannosaurus rex was the biggest meat-eating dinosaur. Its name means 'king of the tyrant reptiles'.

400 T y _ a _ _ o s _ _ r _ s   r _ x

401 Macroplata was a huge reptile that swam in the sea while the dinosaurs walked on the land.

402 M _ c r _ p _ a _ a

403 Baryonyx had a mouth similar to that of a modern-day crocodile, and it caught and ate fish.

404 B a _ y o _ y x

4·05 Quetzalcoatlus was a huge flying creature. Its wingspan was the same as a small aeroplane!

4·06 Q u _ t _ a l c _ a _ l _ s

4·07 Ultrasaurus was one of the tallest of all the dinosaurs – taller than a four-storey building.

4·08 U l _ r _ s a _ _ u s

4·09 Iguanodon got its name because its teeth were shaped like the teeth of a modern-day iguana.

4·10 I g _ a _ o _ o n

Quiz time

Turn to the back of this section for the answers!

Circle the dinosaur names that complete the sentences – look back at the dinosaur gallery to help y

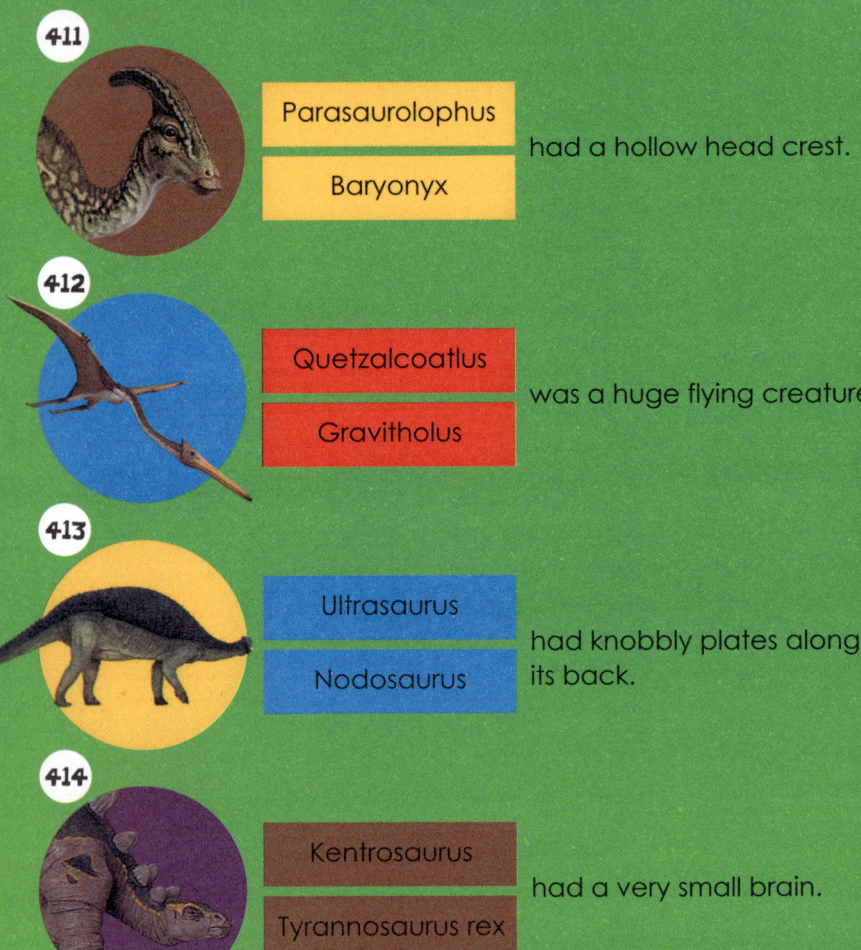

411

Parasaurolophus

Baryonyx

had a hollow head crest.

412

Quetzalcoatlus

Gravitholus

was a huge flying creature.

413

Ultrasaurus

Nodosaurus

had knobbly plates along its back.

414

Kentrosaurus

Tyrannosaurus rex

had a very small brain.

415

Iguanodon

Tyrannosaurus rex

was the biggest meat-eating dinosaur.

416

Triceratops

Nodosaurus

had three sharp horns and a bony frill.

417

Euoplocephalus

Quetzalcoatlus

had a club at the end of its tail.

418

Tyrannosaurus rex

Macroplata

swam in the sea while the dinosaurs walked on the land.

Quiz time

419

Gravitholus

Kentrosaurus

had a thick, heavy skull and may have charged head first.

420

Macroplata

Iguanodon

had teeth shaped like those of a modern-day iguana.

421

Baryonyx

Gravitholus

caught and ate fish.

422

Ultrasaurus

Iguanodon

was taller than a four-storey building.

423 Join the dots to draw the picture of Tyrannosaurus rex.

424 Write the dinosaur's name underneath.

425 Colour in the picture of T-rex.

426 Colour in the frame.

Did you know? T-rex would have been able to gobble up a human being in one gulp!

Quiz answers

411 **Parasaurolophus**

412 **Quetzalcoatlus**

413 **Nodosaurus**

414 **Kentrosaurus**

415 **Tyrannosaurus rex**

416 **Triceratops**

417 **Euoplocephalus**

418 **Macroplata**

419 **Gravitholus**

420 **Iguanodon**

421 **Baryonyx**

422 **Ultrasaurus**

Question time! Of all the dinosaurs, which is your favourite and why?

Velociraptor

Drawing and colouring

Have fun drawing the scenes and colouring them in so they look really great!

 Colour in these flowers when you are ready to start this section.

Making magic

Follow the instructions to make this witch picture look really magical.

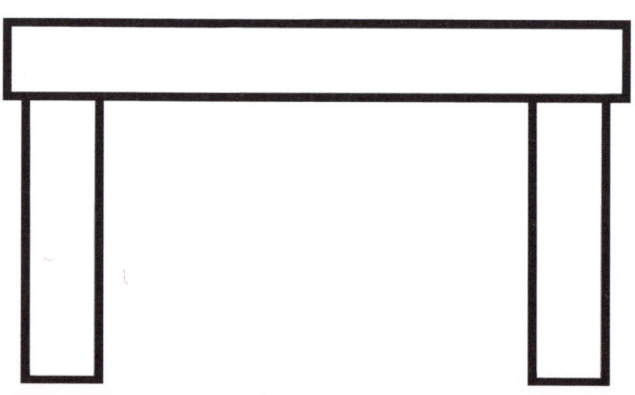

428 Draw a pointy hat on the witch's head.

429 Add a bubbling cauldron to the scene.

430 Give the witch a magic wand to hold.

431 Draw stars around the witch and the cauldron.

432 Draw some magic potions on the table.

433 Colour the witch's dress purple, and her cloak black.

434 Colour the cauldron black, with yellow flames and brown logs.

435 Finish the magical scene by colouring in everything else.

At the show

Emma and her pony Daisy are at the pony show. Can you decorate the scene?

436 Draw a bale of hay next to Daisy.

437 Draw a friendly puppy.

438 Give Emma a stripy riding hat.

439 Add some pretty flowers.

440 Draw a rosette on Daisy's bridle.

441 Colour Daisy whatever colour you like.

442 Add grass to the rest of the scene, and colour it green.

443 Finish the pony show picture by colouring in everything else.

Beautiful butterflies

Can you make this butterfly picture really busy and bright?

444 Draw a large butterfly with a beautiful pattern on its wings.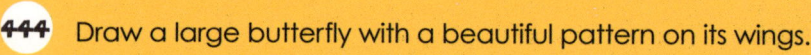

445 Draw another butterfly with a different wing pattern.

446 Add a spotty ladybird to the scene.

447 Draw some pretty flowers.

448 Add bushes to the rest of the scene and colour them green.

449 Make the butterflies really bright and beautiful.

450 Colour the ladybird red with black spots.

451 Finish the butterfly scene by colouring in everything else.

Pirate Scene

Give the pirate some special pirate accessories to make him look really great!

452 Draw a hat on the pirate's head.

453 Cover one of his eyes with an eye patch.

454 Draw a pirate ship in the distance.

455 Draw a skull and crossbones somewhere in the scene.

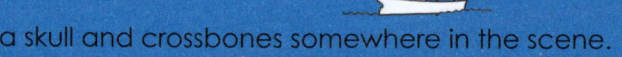

456 Give the pirate a parrot to hold.

457 Colour the parrot in really bright colours.

458 Colour the pirate, and make his hat black.

459 Finish the pirate scene by colouring in everything else.

Hungry rabbits

Can you give the hungry rabbit a friend, and add some more detail to the scene?

460 Draw a friend for the rabbit.

461 Draw a juicy carrot for the rabbits to munch on.

462 Give the rabbits some whiskers.

463 Add a big rainbow to the scene.

464 Draw a large sunflower with lots of petals.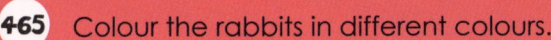

465 Colour the rabbits in different colours.

466 Make the rainbow multicoloured.

467 Finish the rabbit scene by colouring in everything else.

Football time

Follow the instructions to make this football picture look really great.

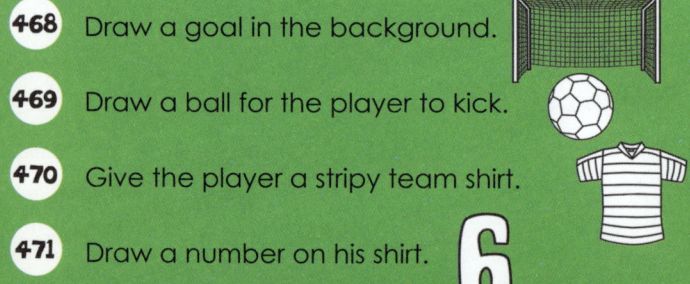

468 Draw a goal in the background.

469 Draw a ball for the player to kick.

470 Give the player a stripy team shirt.

471 Draw a number on his shirt.

472 Add a big sun in the sky.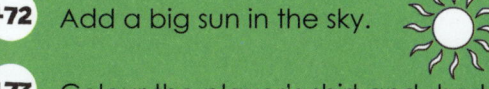

473 Colour the player's shirt and shorts.

474 Colour the sun bright yellow.

475 Finish the football scene by colouring in everything else.

In the sea

Can you make this underwater picture look really busy and colourful?

476 Draw another fish swimming in the sea.

477 Draw a sea horse swimming along.

478 Add a shell and a starfish to the seabed.

479 Draw some bubbles coming out of the fishes' mouths.

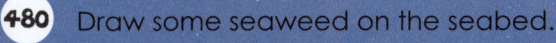

480 Draw some seaweed on the seabed.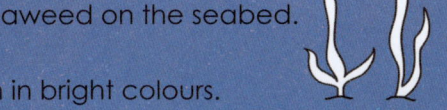

481 Colour the fish in bright colours.

482 Draw the rest of the seabed. Colour it brown, and the water blue.

483 Finish the underwater scene by colouring in everything else.

On safari

Draw some animals and scenery to make this safari scene look amazing.

484 Give the zebra a stripy mane.

485 Draw a sun in the distance.

486 Draw a hippopotamus.

487 Add some trees to the scene.

488 Draw a tall giraffe in the distance.

489 Colour the zebra black and white.

490 Colour in the giraffe and hippopotamus.

491 Finish the safari scene by colouring in everything else.

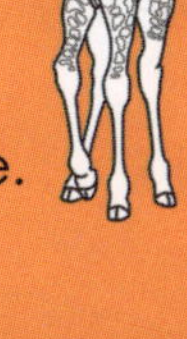

On the farm

Can you add lots of detail to make this farmyard scene look really busy?

492 Draw a shed for the hen to sleep in.

493 Draw a baby chick next to the hen.

494 Add a large sun in the sky.

495 Draw some tufts of grass around the farmyard.

496 Draw a tree in the background.

497 Draw the rest of the farmyard background.

498 Colour the hen and her chick.

499 Finish the farmyard scene by colouring in everything else.

Train scene

Follow the instructions to draw this train travelling through the countryside.

500 Give the train a chimney.

501 Draw some smoke coming out of the chimney.

502 Draw some birds in the sky.

503 Draw the rest of the train track.

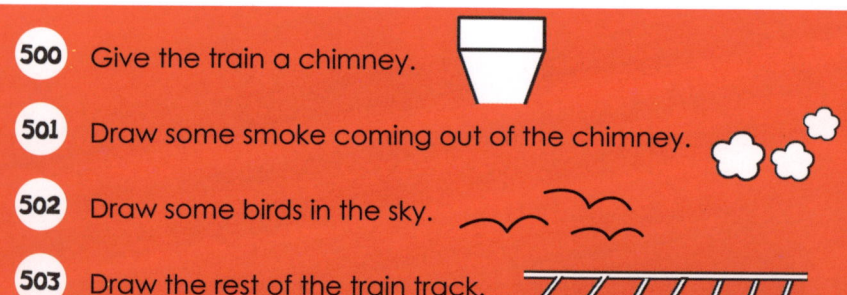

504 Draw some tall trees.

505 Draw the bushes in the background and colour them green.

506 Colour the train whatever colour you like.

507 Finish the train scene by colouring in everything else.

Speedy motorbike

Can you add lots of detail to make this motorbike picture look really fun?

508 Add some detail to the rider's outfit.

509 Draw the wheels on the motorbike.

510 Add some smoke coming out of the exhaust.

511 Draw the road, with a grassy verge.

512 Draw an aeroplane flying in the sky.

513 Colour the motorbike rider so his outfit stands out!

514 Colour the motorbike in a bright colour.

515 Finish the scene by colouring in everything else.

Elephant Scene

Can you add lots of detail to make this elephant scene look really great?

516 Draw some large rocks on the ground.

517 Add some trees to the background.

518 Give the elephant two sharp tusks.

519 Add some spiky grass to the scene.

520 Give the elephant a long tail.

521 Draw the rest of the ground and colour it brown.

522 Colour the elephant grey.

523 Finish the elephant scene by colouring in everything else.

By the pigsty

Can you give the little piglet a friend, and a pigsty for them to play in?

524 Give the piglet a curly tail.

525 Draw a pigsty in the background.

526 Draw a large sun in the sky.

527 Draw a friend for the piglet.

528 Add some straw to the scene.

529 Colour the piglets pink.

530 Colour the straw yellow.

531 Finish the pigsty scene by colouring in everything else.

Nighttime

Add some animals and other things to make this night scene look mysterious.

532 Give the fox a bushy tail.

533 Draw a moon in the sky.

534 Add some stars to the scene.

535 Draw an owl flying in the sky.

536 Draw a cat, fast asleep by the road.

537 Draw the rest of the road and bushes in the background.

538 Colour the fox red or brown.

539 Finish the night scene by colouring in everything else.

Squawking parrots

Can you draw another noisy parrot and make this scene look really colourful?

540 Give the parrot a sharp beak.

541 Draw some flowers on the bushes.

542 Draw a parrot flying in the sky.

543 Draw a big sunflower somewhere in the scene.

544 Add some trees in the background.

545 Draw the rest of the branch and the bushes behind.

546 Colour the parrots in really bright colours.

547 Finish the parrot scene by colouring in everything else.

swimming hippo

Bring this underwater scene to life for the
swimming hippopotamus!

548 Give the hippopotamus a tail.

549 Draw some shells on the seabed.

550 Draw a fish with a crazy pattern.

551 Give your fish a friend.

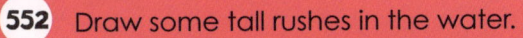

552 Draw some tall rushes in the water.

553 Draw the rest of the seabed and the surface of the water.

554 Colour the hippopotamus whatever colour you like.

555 Finish the scene by colouring in everything else.

Creepy crawlies

Can you draw lots of creepy crawlies to make this scene really busy?

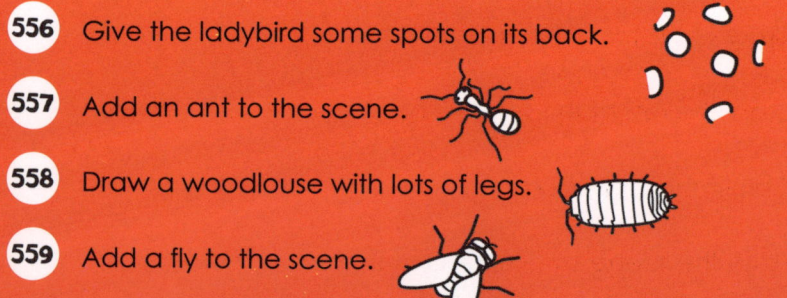

556 Give the ladybird some spots on its back.

557 Add an ant to the scene.

558 Draw a woodlouse with lots of legs.

559 Add a fly to the scene.

560 Draw a big spider.

561 Colour the ladybird red with black spots.

562 Colour the spider brown or black.

563 Finish the creepy crawlie scene by colouring in everything else.

Playful pets

Give Jake the poodle some things to play with, and a friend to share the fun!

564 Give Jake a fluffy tail.

565 Draw a cat friend for Jake.

566 Draw a bone for Jake to chew on.

567 Draw a bed for the animals to sleep in.

568 Add a ball to the scene.

569 Colour the animals whatever colours you like.

570 Make the ball multicoloured.

571 Finish the scene by colouring in everything else.

On the pond

Can you create a pretty pond scene for this friendly frog?

572 Draw some lily pads for the frog to sit on.

573 Add some markings to the frog's body.

574 Draw a flower on one of the lily pads.

575 Add a flying dragonfly to the scene.

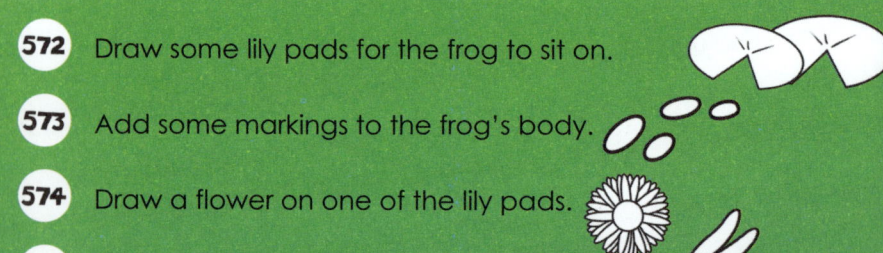

576 Draw some tall rushes in the water.

577 Colour the frog green or brown.

578 Colour the pond water blue.

579 Finish the pond scene by colouring in everything else.

Hot air balloons

Make these hot air balloons really colourful as they fly over the countryside.

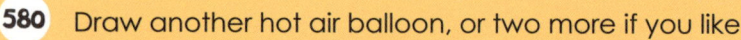

580 Draw another hot air balloon, or two more if you like.

581 Decorate each balloon with a different pattern.

582 Colour the balloons in bright colours.

583 Finish the scene by colouring in everything else.

Puzzle time

Have fun completing lots of amazing puzzles!

584 Colour in the jigsaw puzzle picture when you are ready to start this section.

Seek and find

Look for the toys in the picture that are exactly the same. Circle them when you find them.

585  **586**  **587**   **588**

Colourful shapes

589 Circle the shape that has the most sides.

590 Circle the shape that has the least sides.

591 Colour in the three blank shapes.

What's wrong?

592 Can you circle five things that are wrong with this picture?

Space maze

Find a way through the maze to lead the rocket back to Earth.

Spot the difference

594 Can you spot six differences between these two pictures? Circle these on picture B when you find them.

Sorting shapes

595 Draw lines to match the shapes to their names.

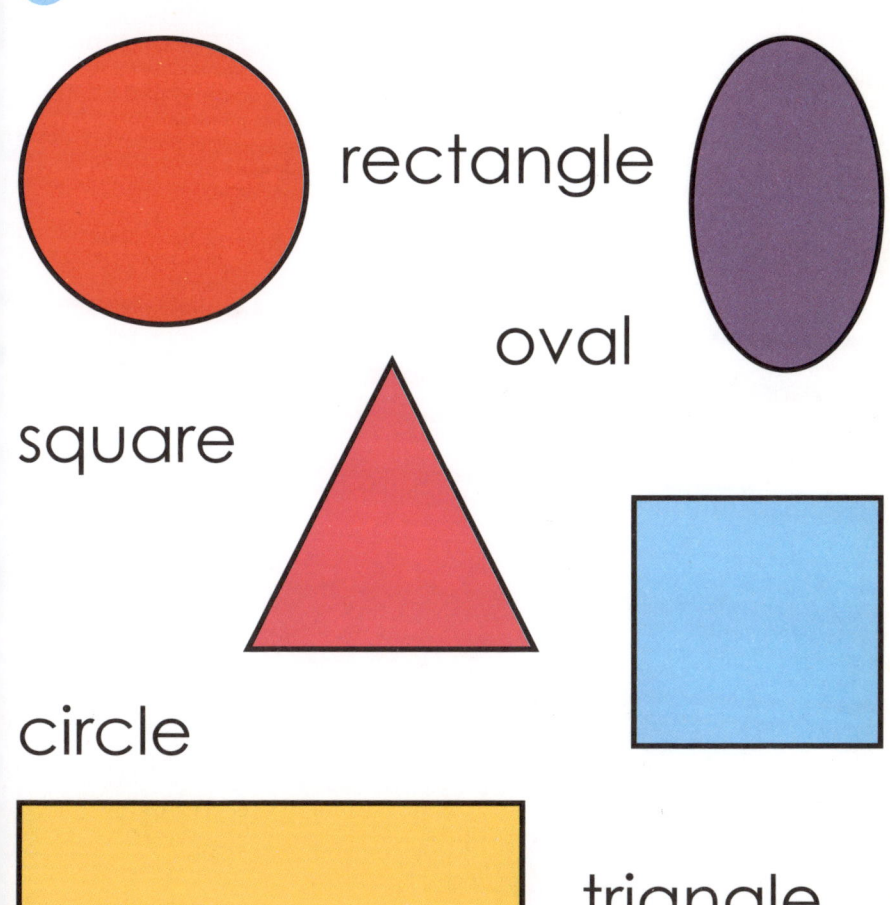

rectangle

oval

square

circle

triangle

Colourful fish

Colour in the fish picture using the coloured spots as a guide.

Rhyme time

Circle the thing in each row that doesn't rhyme with the others.

597 whale   nail   snail   shoe

598 bat   dog   hat   cat

599 coat   cake   boat   goat

600 pan   can   ball   man

Sudoku puzzles

Fill in the numbers 1, 2, 3 or 4 into the empty squares. Each number must appear once in each row, column and box of four squares.

Look at this example:

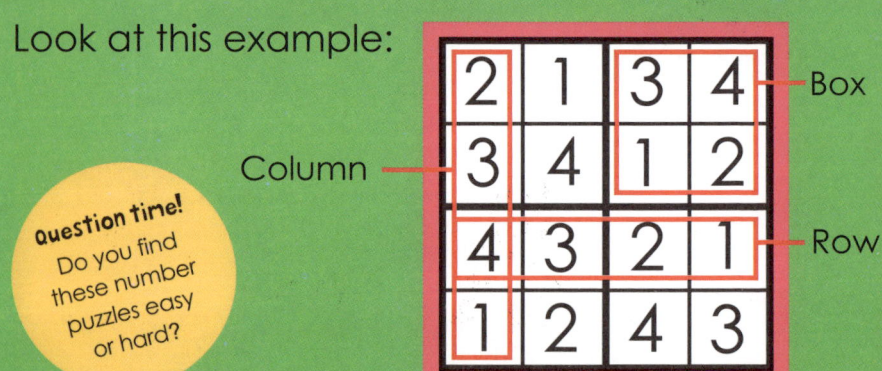

Box

Column

Row

Question time!
Do you find these number puzzles easy or hard?

Now try these sudoku puzzles.

601

	3	1	2
1		3	4
2	1		3
3	4	2	

602

2		1	4
1	4		3
	1		2
4	2		1

603

1	3	2	4
			3
2		3	
3	1	4	2

604

1		3	2
3	2		4
4		2	
	3	4	1

605

	2		1
3		2	4
1	3		2
2		1	3

606

	4		3
3	2		1
4		1	
	1		4

607

3	4		1
2		3	
	2		3
4	3	1	2

608

1			3
2	3		4
3		4	2
	2	3	1

Colour patterns

Colour the pictures to complete the patterns.

609

610

611

612

Dot to dot

613 Join the dots to draw the machine.

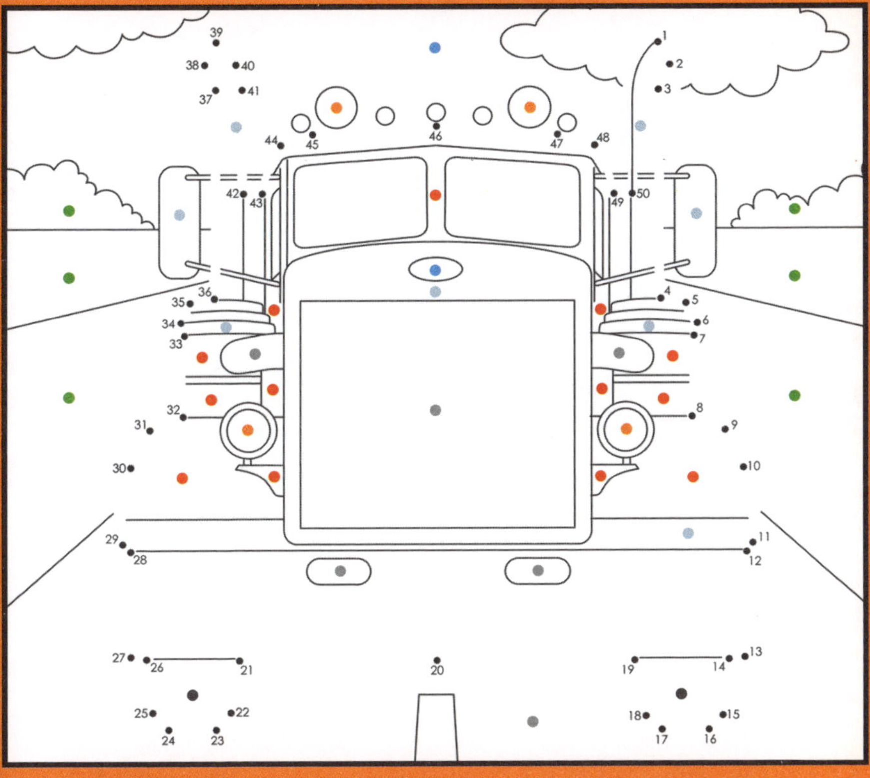

614 Colour in the picture using the coloured dots as a guide.

615 Trace over the name of the machine.

big rig

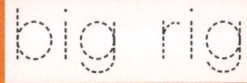

odd one out

Circle the thing in each row that is the odd one out

616   fork   hat   spoon   knife

617   banana   apple   muffin   orange

618   socks   coat   shoes   kite

619   fish   starfish   zebra   octopus

What's wrong?

620 Can you circle five things that are wrong with this picture?

Dot to dot

621 Join the dots to draw the toy.

Question time!
Do you have a favourite toy? What is it?

622 Can you write the name of the toy?

Seek and find

Look for the animals in the picture that are exactly the same. Circle them when you find them.

623 **624** **625** **626**

Making pairs

Circle the things in each row that make a pair.

Spot the difference

631 Can you spot six differences between these two pictures?
Circle these on picture B when you find them.

Colour patterns

Colour the pictures to complete the patterns.

632

633

634

635

Odd one out

Circle the thing in each row that is the odd one out.

636   red flower   pink flower   plant   yellow flower

637   raincoat   flip-flops   rain boots   umbrella

638   basketball   bat   ice cream   tennis racket

639   duckling   bunny   horse   kitten

Seek and find

Look for the things in the picture that are exactly the same. Circle them when you find them.

640 **641** **642** **643**

Matching things

Draw lines between the things that go together.

644

645

646

647

Colourful train scene

Colour in the train picture using the coloured spots as a guide.

missing bug

Circle the bug that is in picture A, but is missing from picture B.

Weather words

Can you use the mixed-up letters to write the weather words?

650 g n h i g n i t l

_ _ _ _ _ _ _ _ _

651 s l c o d u

_ _ _ _ _ _

652 a w b r i n o

_ _ _ _ _ _ _

653 b l a l u r m e

_ _ _ _ _ _ _ _

What's the weather like?

654 Draw a picture to show what the weather is like today.

655 What is your favourite type of weather?

Moo maze

656 Find a way through the maze to lead the cow to her calf.

maths, spelling and more

Practise your maths and spelling, and learn to tell the time.

657 Colour in the clock when you are ready to start this section.

Counting

Count the objects and write the totals.

658   piglets

659   truck

660   apples

661   cupcakes

662   dogs

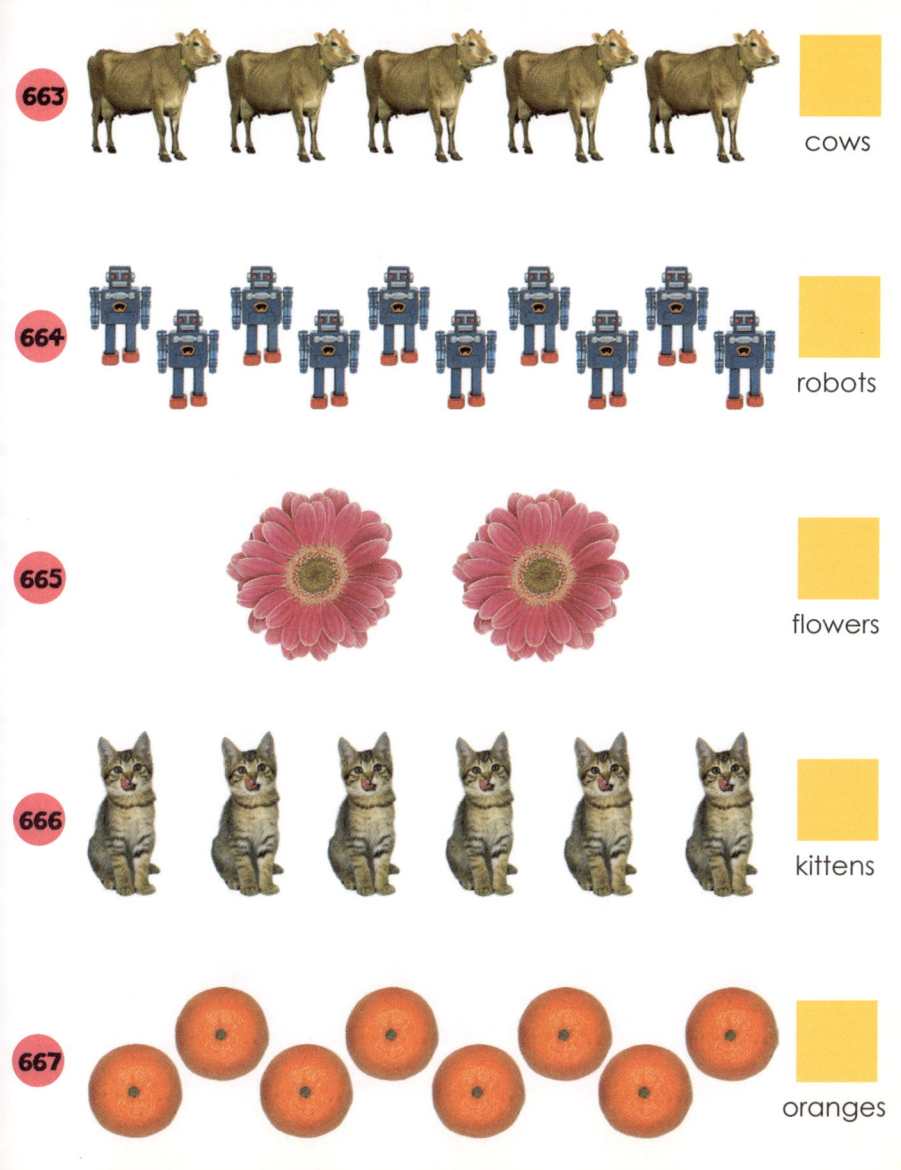

663 cows

664 robots

665 flowers

666 kittens

667 oranges

Adding 1

Add 1 to the first group to find the totals.

 This symbol means "add together"

668 🐄🐄 ➕ 🐄 = 🐄🐄🐄

☐ ☐ ☐

669 🍌🍌🍌 ➕ 🍌 = 🍌🍌🍌🍌

☐ ☐ ☐

670 🐤🐤🐤 ➕ 🐤 = 🐤🐤🐤🐤

☐ ☐ ☐

671 🍁🍁🍁 ➕ 🍁🍁 = 🍁🍁🍁🍁🍁

☐ ☐ ☐

Adding groups

Add the first group to the second group.

672 + =

673 + =

674 + =

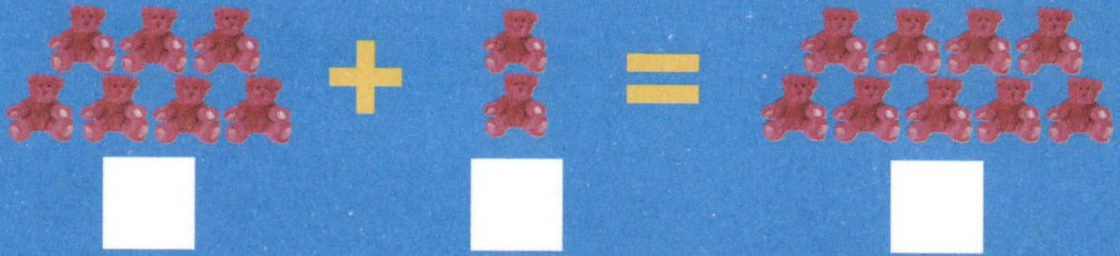

675 + =

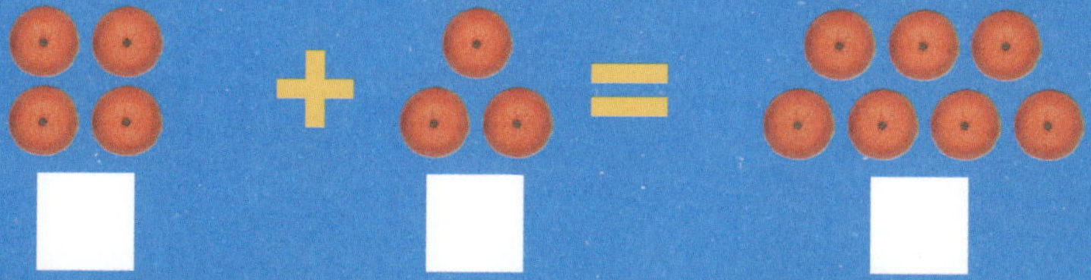

676 + =

Subtracting 1

Take 1 from the first group to find the totals.

🟧 This symbol means "take away"

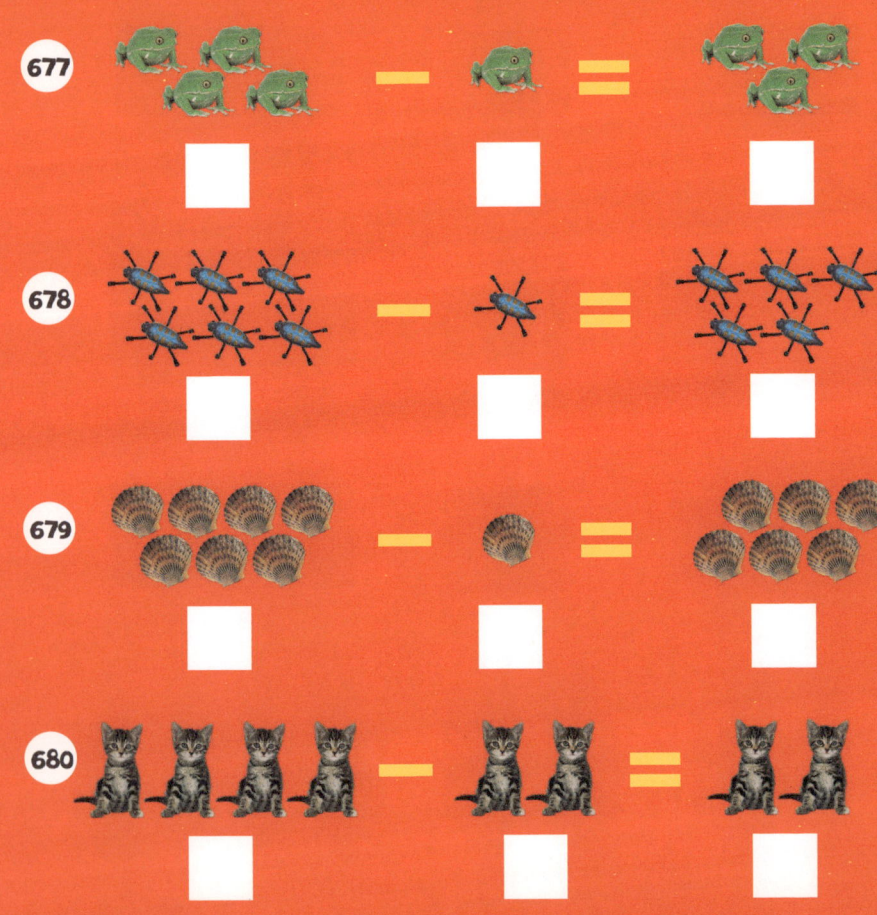

Subtracting groups

Take the second group away from the first group.

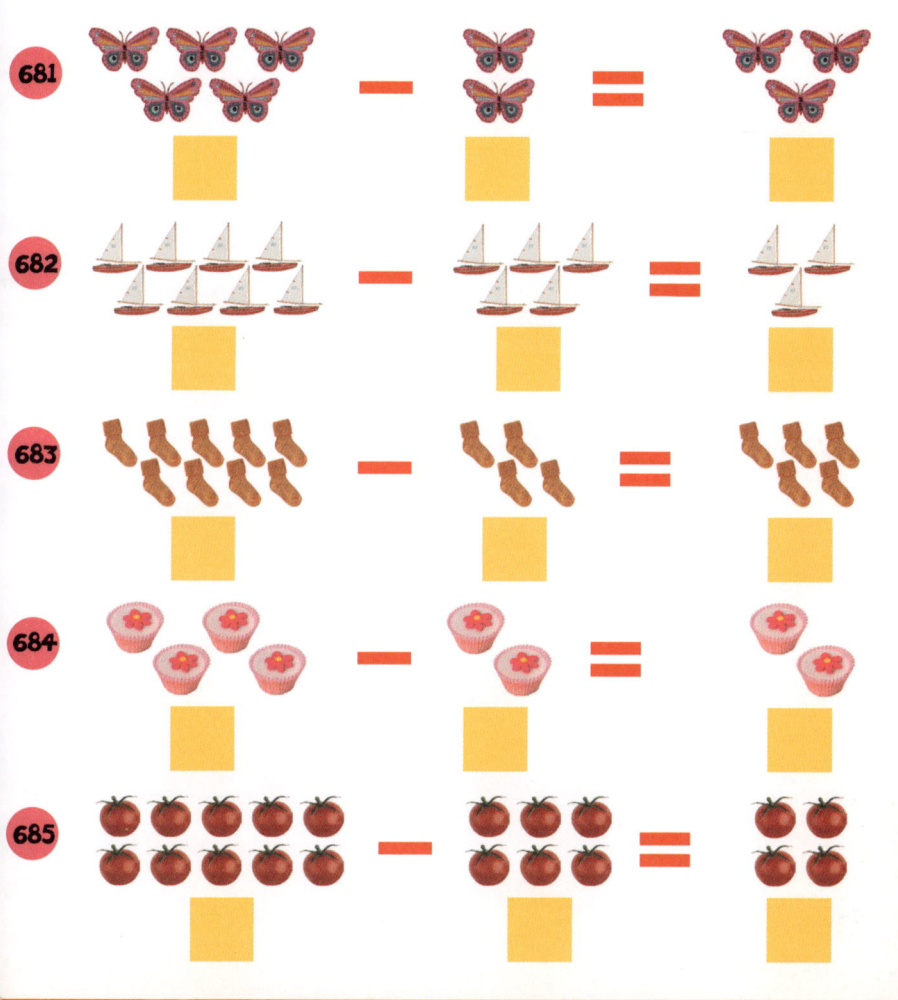

Counting on

Use the counting line to help you add up sums.

To do the sum **2 + 7**, put your finger on **2** and then count forward **7** more numbers. You end on **9**, so **2 + 7 = 9**.

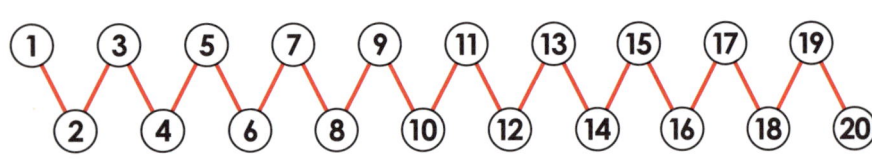

686   3 + 4 = ☐

687   5 + 6 = ☐

688   9 + 3 = ☐

689   1 + 12 = ☐

690   6 + 7 = ☐

691   11 + 4 = ☐

692   13 + 5 = ☐

693   7 + 8 = ☐

694   15 + 3 = ☐

695   11 + 9 = ☐

Counting back

Use the counting line to help you subtract.

To subtract **13 – 5**, put your finger on **13** and then count back **5** numbers. You end on **8**, so **13 – 5 = 8**.

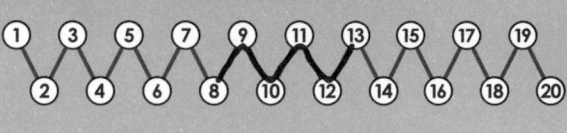

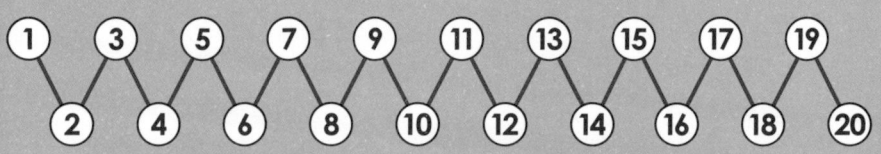

696 9 - 3 =

701 16 - 1 =

697 13 - 8 =

702 14 - 2 =

698 4 - 1 =

703 6 - 3 =

699 7 - 4 =

704 19 - 4 =

700 18 - 5 =

705 20 - 9 =

Doubling numbers

To double a number, add the same number onto itself.

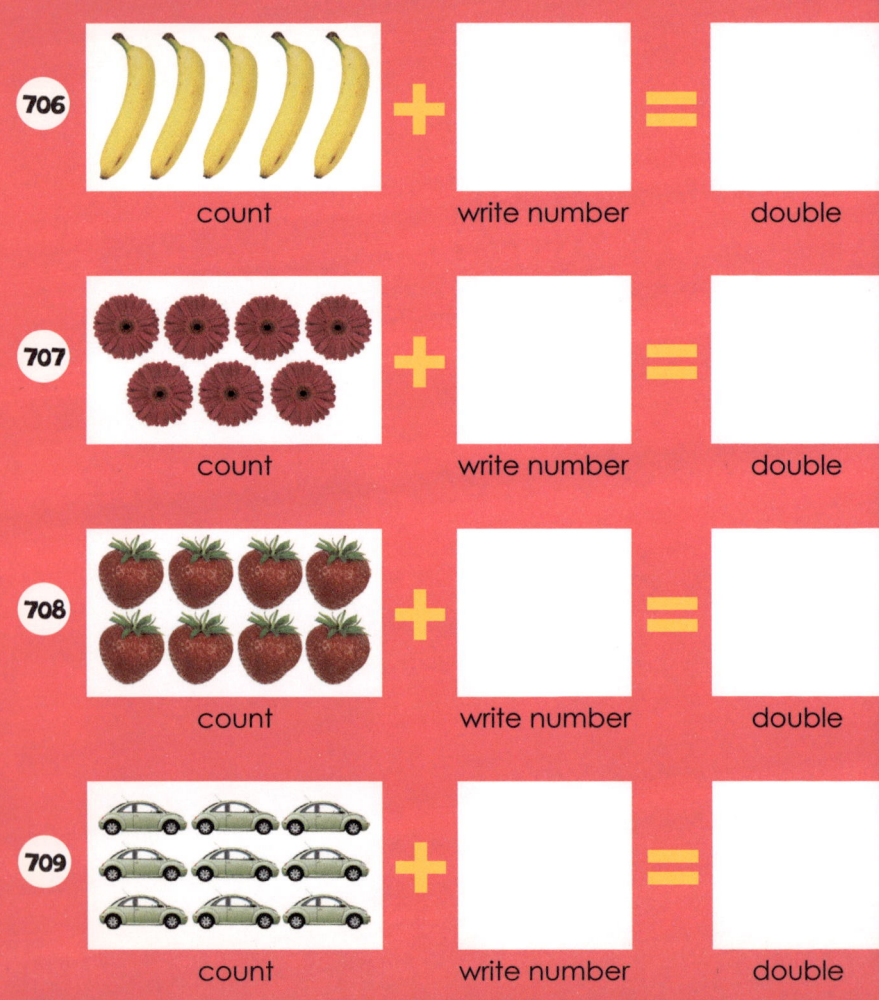

706

count + write number = double

707

count + write number = double

708

count + write number = double

709

count + write number = double

Halving numbers

When you halve a number, the amount you take away is the same number that's left over.

710 Cross out the objects to make **half of 4**

 =

711 Cross out the objects to make **half of 6**

 =

712 Cross out the objects to make **half of 8**

 =

713 Cross out the objects to make **half of 10**

 =

Telling the time

714 Can you trace over the numbers on the clock face below?

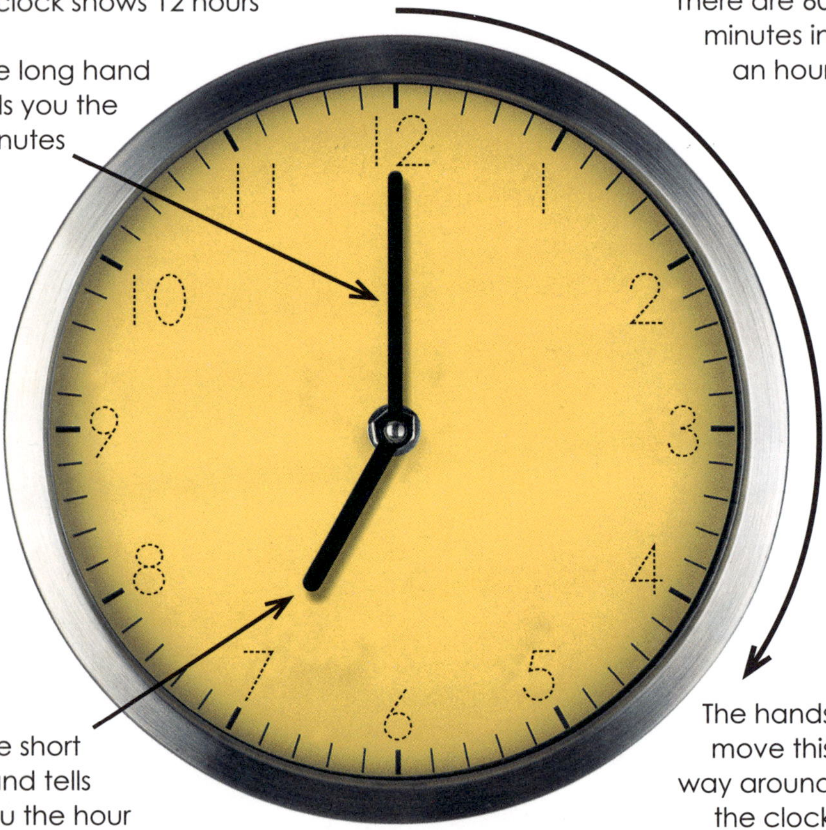
A clock shows 12 hours
There are 60 minutes in an hour
The long hand tells you the minutes
The short hand tells you the hour
The hands move this way around the clock
12
1
2
3
4
5
6
7
8
9
10
11

715 What time does this clock show? ___ o'clock

Write the times that are shown on the clocks.

716 ☐ o'clock

717 ☐ o'clock

718 ☐ o'clock

719 ☐ o'clock

Draw the long and short hands on the clocks.

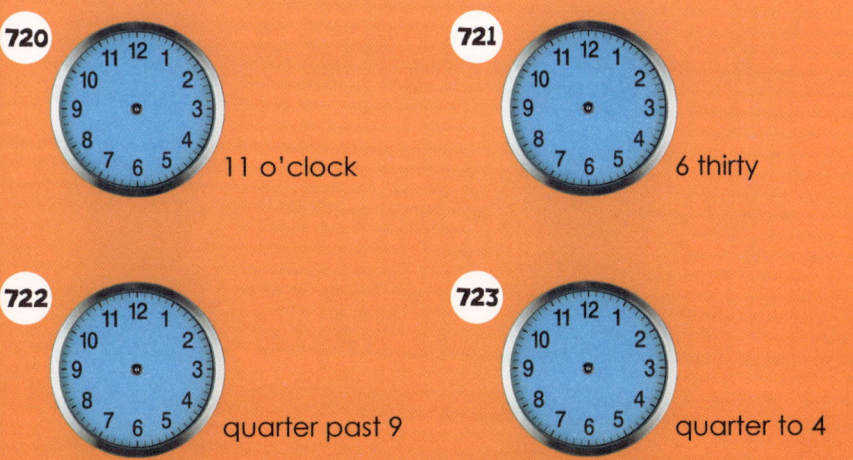

720 11 o'clock

721 6 thirty

722 quarter past 9

723 quarter to 4

What time is it?

Draw the long and short hands on the clocks.

724

10 minutes past 8

725

20 minutes past 10

726

5 minutes to 5

727

10 minutes past 3

728

15 minutes past 9

729

20 minutes to 6

what time do you...?

Show the times of the day that you do these things.

What time do you get up?

What time do you eat breakfast?

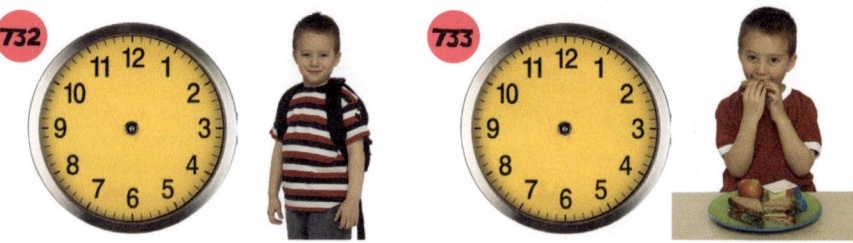

What time do you go to school?

What time do you eat lunch?

What time do you eat dinner?

What time do you go to bed?

Digital time

Digital clocks only use numbers to tell the time.

This clock is showing 4 o'clock. On a digital clock, it is shown as 4:00

Draw the digital and o'clock times on the clocks.

736 3 o'clock 3:00

737 6 o'clock 6:00

738 11 o'clock 11:00

Fill in the o'clock times and the digital times too.

739

☐ o'clock

[:   ]

740

☐ o'clock

[:   ]

741

☐ o'clock

[:   ]

742

☐ o'clock

[:   ]

743

☐ o'clock

[:   ]

744

☐ o'clock

[:   ]

745

☐ o'clock

[:   ]

746

☐ o'clock

[:   ]

747

☐ o'clock

[:   ]

Spelling practice

Fill in the letters that spell these first sounds.

748 __og

749 __ox

750 __ock

751 __ite

752 __ug

753 __orse

754 __uckling

755 __ar

756 __pple

Animal word Search

Fill in the first letters of the animal names, then find the animals in the word search.

757

___ish

c	o	f	t	p	u	p	p	y	e
a	a	i	m	a	c	a	w	j	t
t	e	d	a	n	i	d	r	r	r
e	h	b	m	f	i	a	h	a	f
s	f	r	e	i	n	x	l	b	r
p	i	g	l	s	t	e	a	b	o
i	y	o	a	h	e	m	l	i	a
d	a	t	w	r	g	o	a	t	w
e	q	g	t	g	o	e	k	t	y

758

___at

759

___ig

760

___uppy

761

___abbit

762

___oat

763

___acaw

First sounds

Circle the pictures that begin with the first letters.

764

Circle the things that begin with **t**.

765

Circle the things that begin with **d**.

766

Circle the things that begin with **m**.

Rhyme time

Draw lines between the pictures that rhyme.

767 hat

frog

768 box

bun

769 dog

bat

770 sun

fox

Last letters

Fill in the letters that spell the last sounds.

771 boa__

772 bir__

773 fro__

774 dru__

775 cra__

776 trai__

777 mil__

778 pupp__

779 cu__

Food word search

Fill in the last letters of the food words, then find the foods in the word search.

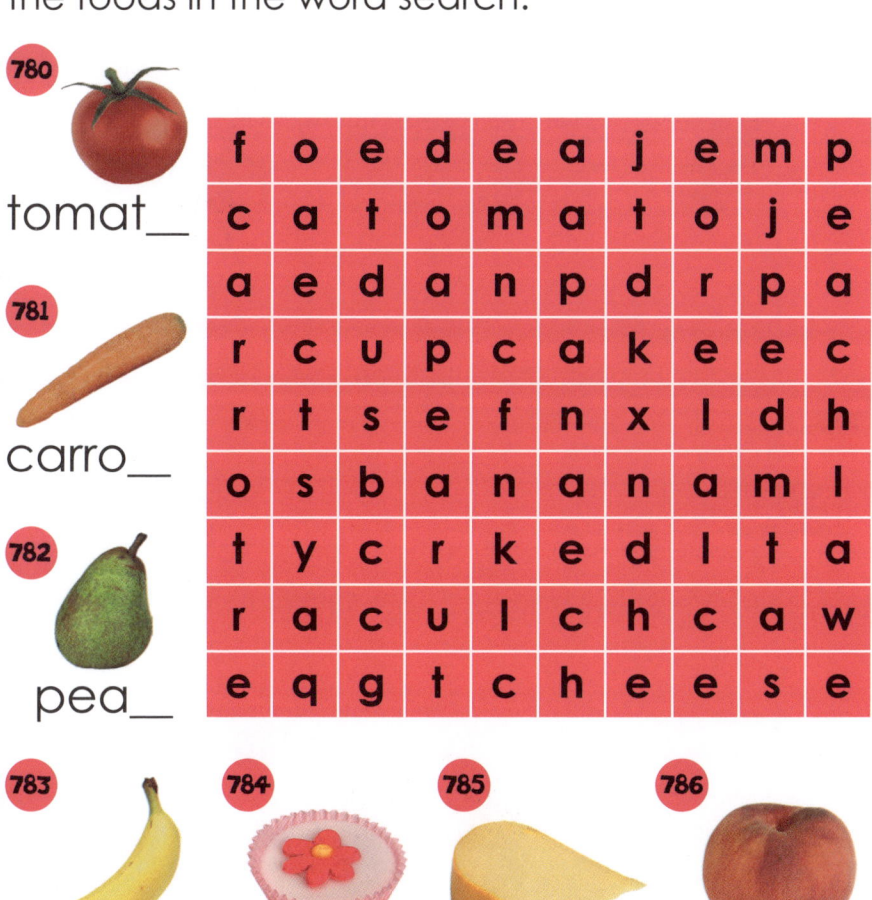

780 tomat__

781 carro__

782 pea__

f	o	e	d	e	a	j	e	m	p
c	a	t	o	m	a	t	o	j	e
a	e	d	a	n	p	d	r	p	a
r	c	u	p	c	a	k	e	e	c
r	t	s	e	f	n	x	l	d	h
o	s	b	a	n	a	n	a	m	l
t	y	c	r	k	e	d	l	t	a
r	a	c	u	l	c	h	c	a	w
e	q	g	t	c	h	e	e	s	e

783 banan__   **784** cupcak__   **785** chees__   **786** peac__

Double letters

Use the double letters **ee** or **oo** to complete the words.

787 b___

788 m___n

789 j___p

790 b___k

791 thr___

792 sh___p

793 w___l

794 wh___l

795 sp___n

Double letters

Use the double letters **pp, tt, dd, rr, ss, mm** or **bb** to complete the words.

796 da___y

797 pu___y

798 ki___

799 bu___les

800 bu___erfly

801 ca___ots

802 mu___y

803 le___ers

804 te___y

Same sounds

Use **ee** or **ea** to make the same sounds in these words.

805 str___t

806 p___ch

807 s___l

808 l___ves

809 s___side

810 asl___p

811 d___r

812 t___th

813 ___gle

Same sounds

Use **ow** or **ou** to make the same sounds in these words.

814 h___se

815 t___el

816 fl___er

817 m___ntain

818 sh___t

819 tr___el

820 sp___t

821 t___er

822 ___l

Missing letters

Fill in the missing letters to spell these words.

823 __ –shirt

824 lea__

825 sh__rts

826 ___gle

827 ca___ots

828 m___ntain

829 lim__

830 __hair

831 bow__

Animal stickers

Learn all about amazing animals, and have fun with lots of stickers.

 832 Colour in the butterfly picture when you are ready to start this section.

on the farm

Find the stickers, then fill in the missing letters to write the names of the farm animals.

P _ _ s

like to play in mud.

D _ _ k _

swim in the pond.

C _ _ s

give us milk.

G _ e _ e

make a "honk" noise.

837

H _ r _ _ s

say "neigh".

838

S _ e _ p

have woolly coats.

839

C _ c k _ r e _ _

say "cock-a-doodle-doo".

840

G _ a _ _

have hairy coats.

841

C h _ _ _ s

are yellow and fluffy.

Farm friends

842 Find the sticker of the donkey.

843 Fill in the missing letters to spell its name.

d _ n _ _ y

844 Circle the trail that leads the duck to her ducklings.

a
b
c

Draw lines to match the animals to what they give us.

845 cow

846 sheep

847 hen

wool

eggs

milk

Find the stickers, then find the farm animals in the word search.

848 lambs

849 goslings

850 llama

851 piglet

852 kid

853 pony

g	k	r	p	g	a	o	l	a	y	g	q	w
b	t	g	o	s	l	i	n	g	s	a	h	f
a	f	o	n	c	a	h	a	p	y	a	w	h
x	s	h	y	u	r	g	w	j	t	f	u	a
o	u	a	g	e	s	k	s	a	v	h	o	p
w	a	m	a	r	y	i	y	l	a	m	b	s
r	b	q	v	u	o	d	u	b	b	j	k	o
h	f	e	p	e	t	m	w	s	o	o	b	l
l	l	a	m	a	f	u	e	t	a	x	w	e
p	e	j	k	e	y	k	a	e	w	t	u	f
t	o	x	t	r	p	a	p	i	g	l	e	t

Speedy animals

Find the stickers, then draw lines to match the animals to the descriptions.

854 Peregrine falcons fly through the sky at super speeds to catch their prey.

855 The cheetah is the fastest animal on land over short distances.

856 An ostrich can run twice as fast as a human sprinter.

857 Dragonflies can hover in one place and fly backwards and forwards.

858 Join the dots to draw the speedy animal.

859 Trace over the letters to spell its name.

860 Find the stickers of the two fish.

did you know?
The sailfish is the fastest fish in the sea!

sailfish

861 Colour in the underwater scene to make it look really great.

Forest Scene

862 Find the sticker of the raccoon.

863 Find the sticker of the porcupine.

falcon

raccoon

fox

wolf

squirrel

864 Find the sticker of the falcon.

865 Which animal is covered in spines?

866 Find the sticker of the owl.

867 Find the sticker of the wolf.

Question time! Which forest animals do you sometimes see in a town?

brown bear

porcupine

owl

868 How many squirrels can you see?

869 What colour is the bear's fur?

Birds

870 Find the sticker of the toucan.

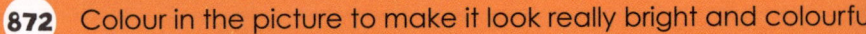

871 Trace over the letters to spell its name.

872 Colour in the picture to make it look really bright and colourful

toucan

Did you know?
Toucans have huge bills, but they are hollow inside so they're not heavy!

Find the stickers, then draw lines to match the birds to the descriptions.

873 Peacocks have large, colourful tails.

874 Seagulls are noisy birds that live by the sea.

875 Parrots can repeat things that people say.

876 Pelicans can carry lots of fish in their bills.

African Scene

877 Find the sticker of the lion.

878 Find the sticker of the elephants.

elephants

hippopotamuses

leopard

879 Find the sticker of the leopard.

880 How many gazelles can you see?

881 Find the sticker of the zebra.

882 Find the sticker of the giraffe.

Question time!
Which of these African animals is your favourite?

gazelles

lion

giraffe

zebras

883 Which animal has a very long neck?

884 How many hippopotamuses are bathing in the water?

In Africa

Find the stickers, then use the mixed-up letters to write the names of the African animals.

885 _ _ _ _ _
a e b r z

886 _ _ _ _ _ _ _
e f f g r i a

887 _ _ _ _ _
c l e m a

888 _ _ _ _
o l i n

889 Join the dots to draw the African animal.

890 Trace over the letters to spell its name.

891 Find the stickers of the two rhinoceroses.

Did you know? A rhino's horn is made from tightly-packed hairs – there's no bone!

892 Colour in the rhinoceros scene.

Amazing defence

893 Some butterflies hide themselves in bright flowers. Find the sticker, then colour the flowers to match the butterfly.

894 Find a way through the maze for the butterfly to reach the colourful flowers.

Find the stickers, then circle the words that complete the sentences.

895 Hippopotamuses defend themselves using their sharp...

teeth / feet

896 Octopuses squirt black ink into the water to make their enemies...

happy / confused

897 Poison dart frogs release poison through their skin to make them taste...

delicious / nasty

898 Reindeer fight each other with their large...

antlers / toes

How old am I?

Find the stickers, then trace over the names of the animals.

899 Goldfish

live for about eight years – a long time for a fish!

900 Mayflies

only live for about two hours.

901 Lobsters

live for about 80 years.

902 Crocodiles

can live for up to 100 years.

903 Find the sticker of the giant tortoise.

904 Can you spot six differences between these two giant tortoises? Circle these on picture B.

A

B

Did you know?
The Galapagos giant tortoise can live for over 200 years.

Ocean Scene

905 Find the sticker of the octopus.

906 Find the sticker of the yellow fish.

dolphin

octopus

yellow fish

sea horses

starfish

907 Which sea creature is crawling along the seabed?

908 How many arms does the starfish have?

909 Find the sticker of the shark.

910 Find the sticker of the sea turtle.

Question time! How many of these sea creatures have you seen?

whale

shark

crab

sea turtle

911 Which sea creature is only showing its tail above the water?

912 Which sea creature is your favourite?

In the sea

913 Circle the trail that leads the penguin to her chicks.

a
b
c

Find the stickers, then fill in the missing letters to write the names of the sea creatures.

914

c _ _ _

915

d o _ _ _ i _

916

w h _ _ _

917

f _ _ _

Find the stickers, then find the sea creatures in the word search.

e	k	w	p	g	a	p	e	n	g	u	i	n
b	t	a	g	r	a	t	c	n	g	a	h	f
p	o	l	a	r	b	e	a	r	y	j	w	h
x	s	r	h	u	r	g	w	j	t	e	u	a
o	u	u	g	e	s	n	s	a	v	l	o	p
w	a	s	e	a	l	q	y	g	n	l	g	c
r	b	q	v	u	o	h	u	m	b	y	k	o
h	f	e	p	d	e	l	w	s	o	f	b	l
g	c	n	y	g	f	u	e	t	a	i	w	e
p	s	e	a	h	o	r	s	e	w	s	r	f
t	o	x	t	r	p	a	m	n	h	h	g	o

918
jellyfish

919
penguin

920
sea horse

921
walrus

922
polar bear

923
seal

Parents and babies

Find the stickers, then draw lines to match the parents to their babies.

924 elephant

baby
orangutan

925 kangaroo

seal
pup

926 orangutan

elephant
calf

927 seal

kangaroo
joey

Find the stickers, then draw lines to match the parents to their babies.

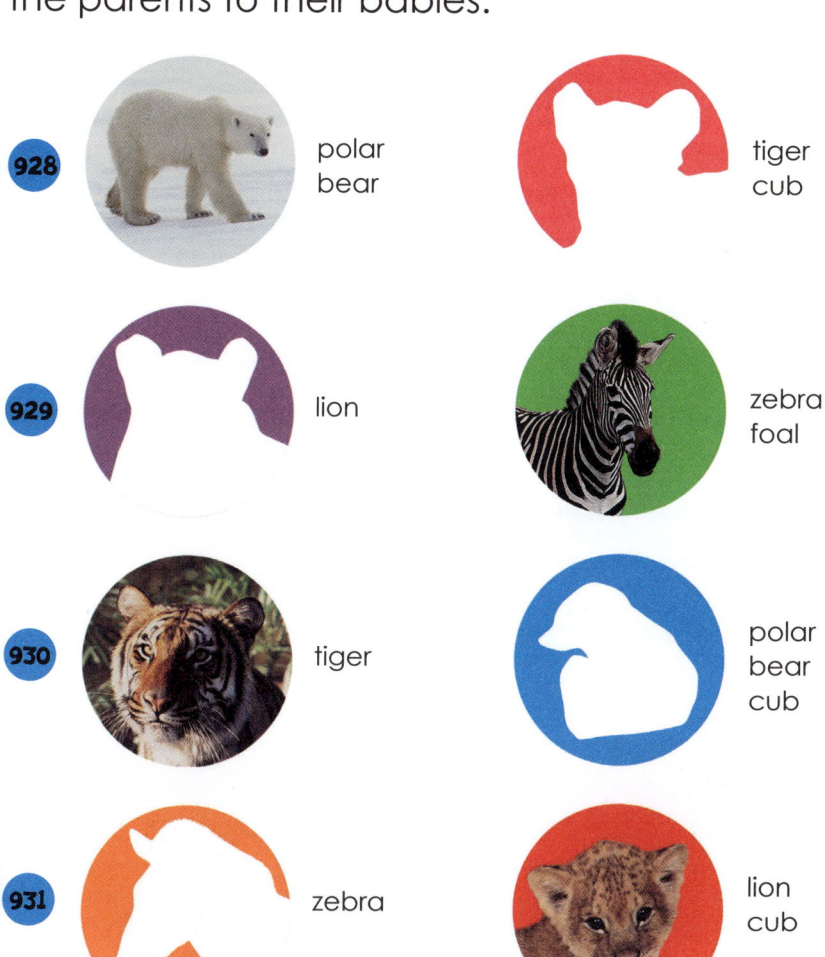

928 polar bear

tiger cub

929 lion

zebra foal

930 tiger

polar bear cub

931 zebra

lion cub

In the jungle

932 Find the sticker of the spider.

933 Only two spiders are exactly the same. Can you circle which two?

934 Fill in the missing letters to spell its name.

Did you know?
Most spiders have eight eyes, but they have very poor eyesight!

a

b

c

d

e

f

s _ _ _ e _

Find the stickers, then find the jungle animals in the word search.

 **935**
parrot

 936
snake

 937
panda

 938
tiger

 **939**
gorilla

940
iguana

f	k	r	a	t	r	f	w	h	a	i	v	g
b	t	t	m	v	y	r	m	r	g	a	h	f
a	f	i	g	w	a	h	a	h	y	a	w	h
x	s	g	o	r	i	l	l	a	t	f	u	a
o	u	e	g	i	s	e	s	a	v	h	o	p
w	a	r	a	r	y	i	y	e	r	e	p	e
s	b	q	v	u	o	e	u	b	f	j	a	o
n	f	e	p	a	r	r	o	t	o	o	n	l
a	e	r	i	e	f	u	e	t	a	x	d	e
k	e	j	k	r	y	i	g	u	a	n	a	f
e	o	x	t	r	p	a	v	w	e	m	a	e

Creepy crawlies

Find the stickers, then use the mixed-up letters to write the names of the creepy crawlies.

941

_ _ _ _ _ _

p s i e d r

942

_ _ _ _ _

n i s a l

943

_ _ _ _ _ _

e t e b l e

944

_ _ _ _

m o w r

945

_ _ _ _

h t m o

Question time!
Which creepy
crawlie has a
hard shell on
its back?

946

_ _ _

e b e

947

_ _ _ _ _ _ _ _ _

o o d w e o u s l

948

_ _ _

n t a

949

_ _ _ _ _ _ _

r i c k c t e

Creepy crawlie scene

950 Find the sticker of the dragonfly.

951 Find the sticker of the grasshopper.

butterfly

dragonfly

caterpillar

wasp

snail

ant

952 Find the sticker of the fly.

953 Which creepy crawlie has black spots on its back?

954 Find the sticker of the spider.

955 Find the sticker of the snail.

Question time!
Which creepy crawlie makes tasty honey?

bee

fly

ladybird

spider

grasshopper

956 Which creepy crawlie has really long legs?

957 Which creepy crawlies are eating an apple?

Amazing animals

958 Find the sticker of the crocodile.

959 Fill in the missing letters to spell its name.

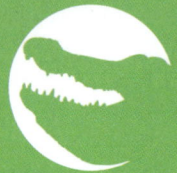

c _ o _ _ _ i _ _

960 Ostriches are unusual animals because their eyes are bigger than their brains! In the pictures below, only two ostriches are exactly the same – can you circle which two?

Did you know?
Saltwater crocodiles can survive up to two years in between meals!

A

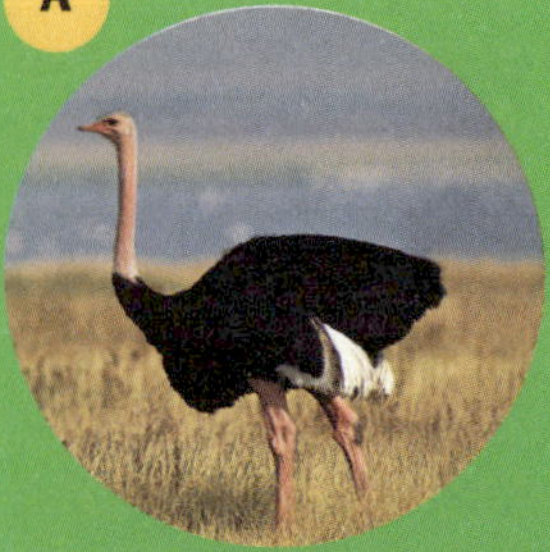

B

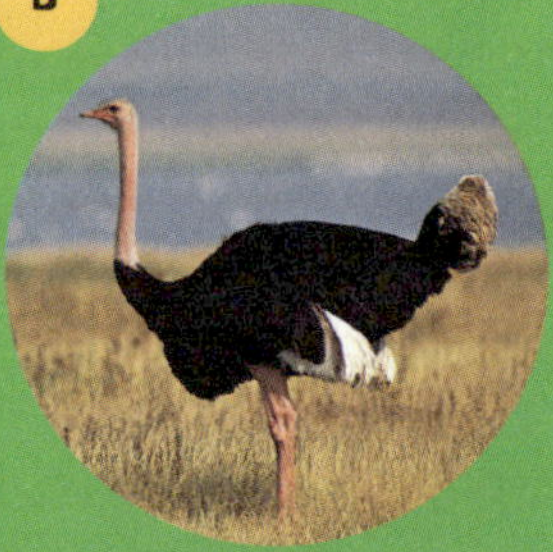

C

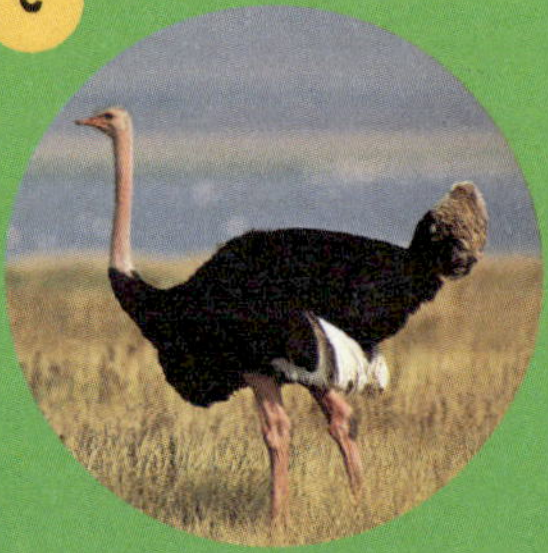

D

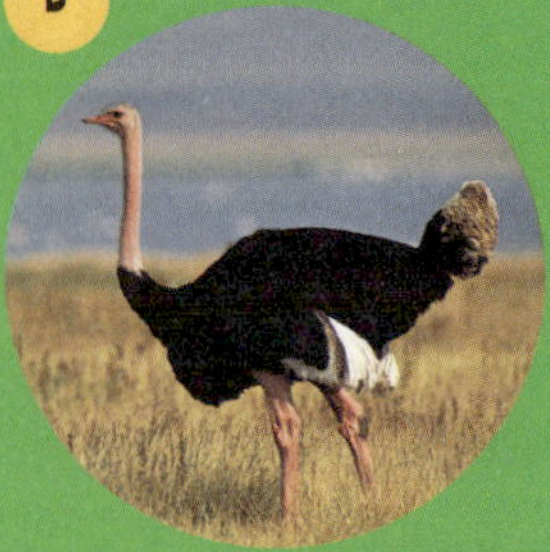

E

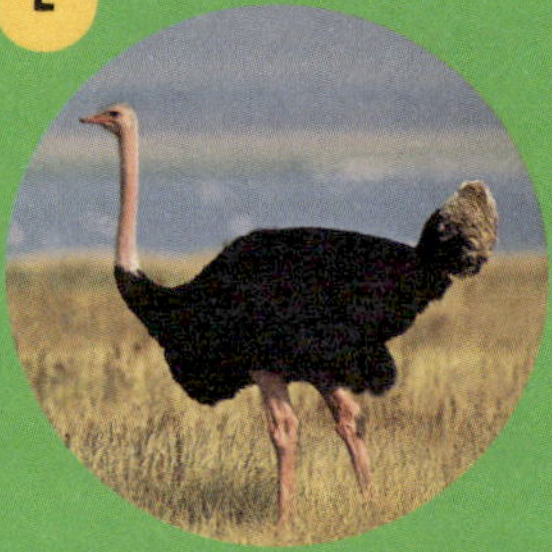

F

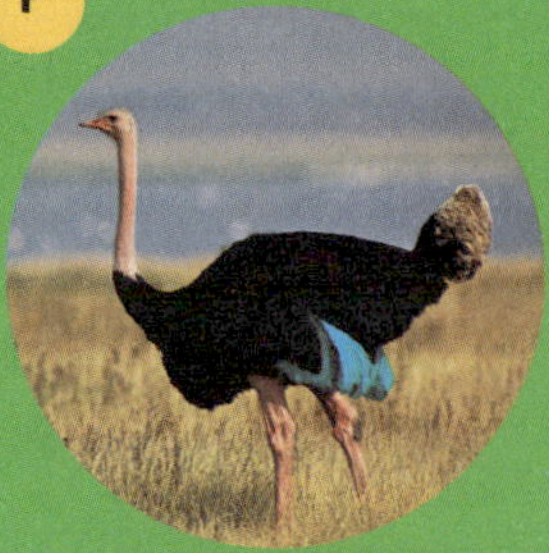

Find the stickers, then circle the words that complete the sentences.

961 Sharks have an excellent sense of smell and a good sense of hearing. They are very...

fierce / friendly

962 Black widow spiders are small, but have a bite that is very...

tiny / poisonous

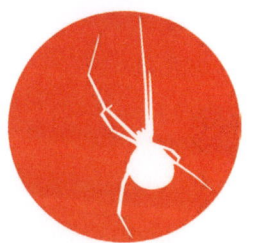

963 Hummingbirds beat their wings up to 75 times each second. This is what makes the humming...

noise / dance

964 Yaks can survive in temperatures as low as -40° Celcius. Their coats are very...

colourful / hairy

Record breakers

Find the stickers, then trace over the names of the record-breaking animals.

965 Camels

are able to survive without water for two weeks.

966 Blue whales

are the biggest animals in the world. Their tongues weigh as much as an elephant!

967 Elephants

have tusks that act like their front teeth. These tusks grow around 20 cm each year.

968 Giraffes

are the tallest animals in the world. Most of their height is in their necks.

969 Find the sticker of the tiger.

970 Join the dots to draw the picture.

971 Trace over the letters to spell its name.

tiger

Did you know?
A tiger's roar can be heard from about 2 km away!

972 Colour in the tiger picture.

Pets

Find the stickers, then use the mixed-up letters to write the names of the pets.

973

_ _ _ _ _ _

t a r p o r

974

_ _ _ _ _ _   _ _ _

u e a n i g   g p i

975

_ _ _ _ _ _

i t r a b b

976

_ _ _ _ _ _ _ _

h s f i o l g d

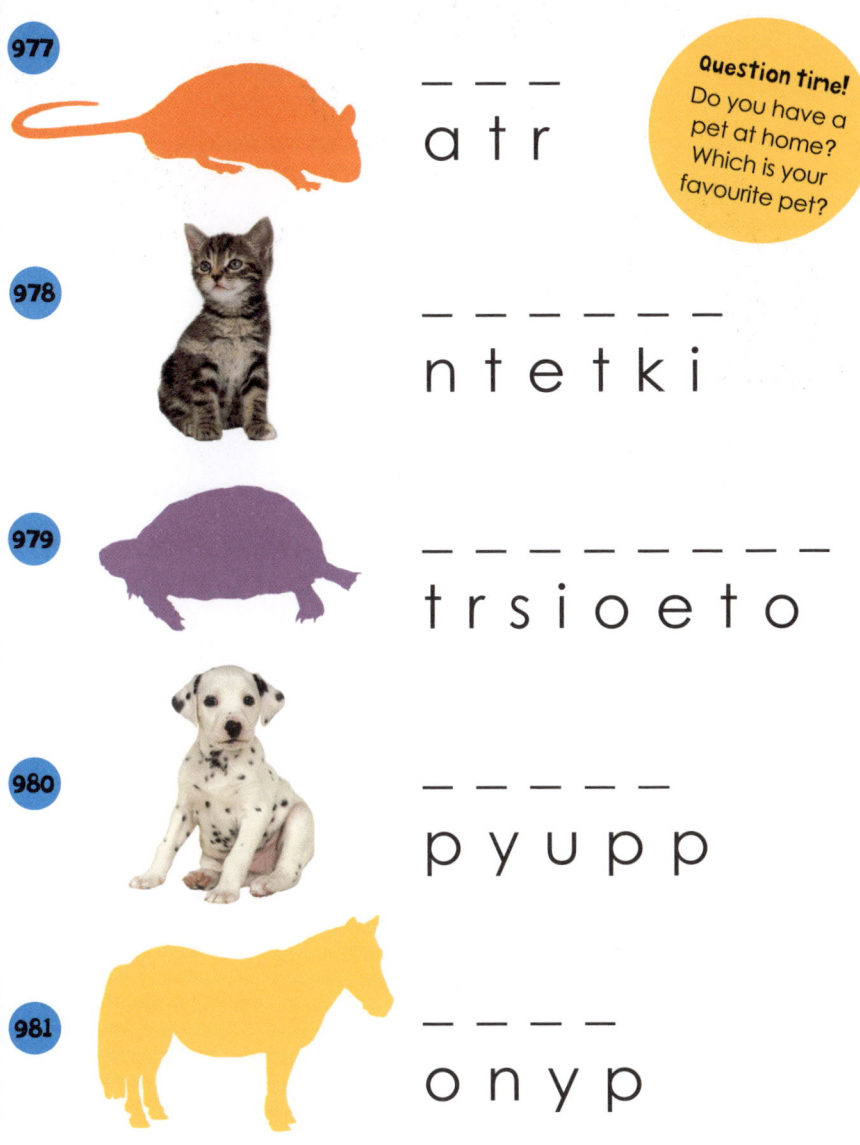

977 _ _ _

a t r

Question time!
Do you have a
pet at home?
Which is your
favourite pet?

978 _ _ _ _ _ _

n t e t k i

979 _ _ _ _ _ _ _ _

t r s i o e t o

980 _ _ _ _ _

p y u p p

981 _ _ _ _

o n y p

Perfect pets

982 Circle the trail that leads the cat to her kittens.

a
b
c

983 Find the sticker, then find a way through the maze to help the mouse reach the cheese.

Find the stickers, then find the pets in the
word search.

g	k	o	p	r	a	d	p	y	m	r	j	k
b	p	d	g	m	k	g	h	g	g	a	h	f
p	u	y	p	p	a	r	a	k	e	e	t	h
x	p	o	j	u	r	g	m	j	t	p	u	a
o	p	m	g	e	s	y	s	a	v	o	o	p
w	i	p	s	r	k	g	t	g	c	a	t	g
r	e	q	v	u	p	m	e	b	b	p	k	o
h	s	e	p	d	o	l	r	s	o	d	b	l
g	t	g	s	j	p	u	e	t	a	o	w	e
p	f	j	m	o	u	s	e	p	s	g	p	f
t	e	x	t	i	r	a	s	r	g	p	r	y

984
dog

985
hamster

986
puppies

987
cat

988
parakeet

989
mouse

Australian scene

990 Find the sticker of the emu.

991 Find the sticker of the kookaburra.

kangaroos

emu

992 Find the sticker of the kangaroo.

993 Which animal is standing with its baby?

994 Find the sticker of the wallaby.

995 Find the sticker of the tarantula.

kookaburra

koala

wallaby

wombats

tarantula

996 Which animal is asleep in the tree?

997 Which Australian animal is your favourite?

on the reef

998 Find the sticker of the reef scene.

999 Trace over the letters to spell the name.

1000 Colour the fish and the rest of the reef scene in bright colours.

reef

Did you know?
Many fish and other animals make their homes on and around the reef.